The Yorkshire Dales

The Yorkshire Dales

Local and Family History

George Redmonds

Wharncliffe Books

First published in Great Britain in 2011 by
WHARNCLIFFE BOOKS
An imprint of
Pen & Sword Books Ltd
47 Church Street
Barnsley
South Yorkshire
S70 2AS

ISBN 978-1-84563-140-6

Typeset by Concept, Huddersfield, West Yorkshire
Printed and bound in England by CPI UK

Pen & Sword Books Ltd incorporates the imprints of Pen & Sword Aviation, Pen & Sword Family History, Pen & Sword Maritime, Pen & Sword Military, Pen & Sword Discovery, Wharncliffe Local History, Wharncliffe True Crime, Wharncliffe Transport, Pen & Sword Select, Pen & Sword Military Classics, Leo Cooper, The Praetorian Press, Remember When, Seaforth Publishing and Frontline Publishing.

For a complete list of Pen & Sword titles please contact
PEN & SWORD BOOKS LIMITED
47 Church Street, Barnsley, South Yorkshire, S70 2AS, England
E-mail: enquiries@pen-and-sword.co.uk
Website: www.pen-and-sword.co.uk

Contents

Acknowledgments

Over the last twenty-five years I have been privileged to conduct parties of American genealogists and historians on tours of the Yorkshire Dales, some of them on foot. Twice in that period groups of Cowgills from the USA, descendents of a Quaker emigrant of the late seventeenth century, have spurred me on to discover the source of their very Yorkshire surname and that task was finally completed in 2006. The tour that year inspired me to write this book and I hope that in it I have captured some of the fascination that the Dales landscape holds for me and for such visitors. Some of the illustrations I have used are from my own collection or are photographs taken by my wife Ann-Marie and her brother Tony Burke: others I owe to American friends who accompanied me round the Dales or took me to places in the USA linked with Yorkshire families, and I am delighted here to acknowledge their help and their many contributions. Thank you therefore, Meriwether Schmid, Perry Cowgill, the late Paula Gmelch, Sandi Hewlett, Lee Nettnin and Peter Van Demark. Thank you also to Brian Elliott for his help in preparing this publication.

The Dales: the lane from Malham to Gordale and Lee Gate, an ancient way between two contrasting landscapes. (Peter Van Demark)

Introduction

In any Yorkshire bookshop there are likely to be several publications with 'Yorkshire Dales' in the title, a clear indication of the attraction that this region has for the public, and the inspiration that it has offered to writers on many subjects. Nevertheless, there are some topics that have received very little attention and that has persuaded me to add another title to the Dales' bibliography. The emphasis in these pages will be on name studies and family history, using them I hope to shed new light on the landscape and the people of the Dales. I take advantage of much new primary source material, particularly title deeds, court rolls and the records of the old Quarter Sessions, and seek to integrate that with what we already know about the region. The book will have served its purpose if it persuades readers of the value that names and lexical items more generally have for local and family historians.

On that theme, I now raise two points that have been inspired by the choice of the title, for I was surprised to discover that the Oxford English Dictionary (OED) has no entry for 'Yorkshire Dales', although Yorkshire ale, Yorkshire Relish and Yorkshire terrier are a few of the numerous other items defined under 'Yorkshire'. The first point relates to a line in T.D. Whitaker's *History of Craven*, to give that mammoth work its short title. In 1812 the author wrote of Littondale that it was 'more anciently and properly Amerdale', a name which he claimed derived from 'Amer, Almer, Aylmer or Almeric ... its first planter in Saxon times'. Wordsworth mentioned the 'deep fork of Amerdale' in the *White Doe of Rylstone* just a few years later and thereafter the name captured the attention of numerous writers. Edmund Bogg called it 'classic Amerdale' in 1921 and quoted Wordsworth; Halliwell Sutcliffe used the name consistently in *Striding Dales* (1929), rejoicing that 'a name so happy could have been coined by alchemy of ancient folk speech'. And yet I have found no reference to Amerdale in any of the documents that I have studied, and I wonder how and where it came to Whitaker's attention. Similarly, I find no mention of Yoredale in the documentary evidence although examples of the river name with that spelling, or something similar, are on record from the sixteenth century. There is no entry for either Amerdale or Yoredale in Smith's volumes on Yorkshire place-names and yet forms of Littondale and Wensleydale have appeared regularly from the twelfth century.

Several other place-names which have -dale as a suffix capture our attention because the element has replaced the Anglian -denu, a word which had much the same meaning. Perhaps the best example is Lothersdale, 'the beggar's valley', spelt Lodresdene in 1086 and Lothersden in 1540. In 1589 we find 'Lothersdaill alias Loddersden' and thereafter the original spelling soon fell out of fashion. Similarly, Arkendale near Knaresborough was originally Arkenden. Colloquially -denu survived as the word 'dean' but perhaps speakers did not associate that word with the place-name element and -dale was preferable because of its transparent meaning.

More recently Ella Pontefract and Marie Hartley had a chapter on 'Bishopdale and Waldendale' in their book on Wensleydale (1936) but I suspect that they coined the name Waldendale for the sake of euphony since I find no reference to it in Yorkshire records. Whether or not that is the case, it is surely a strange name, for it contains both -denu and -dale which have the same meaning. It reminds us of other Dales names that have the Anglian suffix, notably Buckden, Hebden and Keasden and these are evidence of a layer of names much older than those which have a Scandinavian origin. Information of this kind suggests that enquiries into the use and significance of even the most straightforward name elements are likely to turn up interesting data and new lines of research.

The second topic touches on the history of the term 'Yorkshire Dales' which is likely to have grown in importance since the creation of the National Park but may have its roots in a much earlier period. It was usual in the past for a man to refer to the district in which he lived as his 'country' and for the outsider that might even be the name of the shire. For example, in a book on husbandry of 1523 the writer commented on the different kinds of plough that were traditionally used in 'Lankesshyre, Yorkeshyre … and manye other countreyes'. More typically 'country' was a term employed of a much smaller region, as when the abbot of Fountains leased land to William Thornton of Halton Gill and placed him under the supervision of the abbey's officer 'in that countreth' (1511). When George Carter of Grinton wrote his will, in 1547, he had responsibilities in mind for his son Jeffrey when he came back 'into the countre' – indicating that he was temporarily away from Swaledale. Similarly, the will of William Hardcastle of Lofthouse in Nidderdale (1611) outlined his plans for a man called Peter Todd if he should 'make his returne into the countrey'. It might be inferred that these 'countries' were the upper regions of Littondale, Swaledale and Nidderdale and if that were so the idea that 'The Dales' were in themselves a region seems unlikely.

Nevertheless, there is one important reference in that period which might indicate that there was a growing awareness of the Dales as a region among the dalesmen themselves. In a Chancery case of 1562–65, which concerned the lords of Healaugh in Swaledale and their tenants, several ancient men were called on to give evidence about the customs in that manor. More than once reference was made to the system of tenant right and how it operated in Swaledale and 'other places ... named and termed Dales, as Rysendall, Wensidale, Coverdale, Archedale and divers others like'. When the discussion moved on to the liability that tenants had to serve on the Scottish border in defence of the realm, mention was made of 'places and precincts within Yorkshire termed Dales'. Edward Mylner of Muker aged 'four score years and more' spoke of tenant right as a custom 'had and used ... by the inhabitants of Wensley daile, Arkendale, Dentt and Sedbire': Ralph Mylner said 'the like custom' applied also to Bishopdale and Coverdale.

In some respects therefore the dalesmen in Swaledale were already conscious under the Tudors that they belonged to a wider community. Their wills are evidence that partible inheritance was the custom in that community, not primogeniture, and the lands they farmed were held by tenant right and the customary payment of gressoms. Perhaps more importantly they were obliged to follow their lords to the Scottish border 'furnished with bowe and arrows or bill with Jack and Sallet'. When the tenant right issue was raised again, in 1612, the tenants were said to live 'in a mountainous country adjoining unto Westmorland and have very barren grounds'. In the past their ancestors' estates had 'been spoiled with many incursions and robberies'. The clear inference is that dalesmen had been united by their customs, the harsh landscape in which they lived and the threat of a common danger.

Chapter 1

Landscape and Place-Names

The emphasis in place-name studies was formerly on the etymology of the most important settlement sites, and scholars used that information to discover more about the local topography and the early history of successive waves of invaders, especially the Anglians, Danes and Norwegians. And yet those names are far outnumbered by the names which were coined in the Middle English period, as the native language was modified by the French of the invading Normans and local dialects developed. More importantly there is often evidence from that period which relates to the circumstances in which the names were coined, and that allows us to define the place-name elements in their local context.

Most place-name elements feature in the standard works of reference but the entries can rarely take account of all the regional distinctions, so it is a field of research open to the discerning local historian. Numerous elements still await the special attention they deserve so a few will be examined here in detail, in order to demonstrate the possibilities of this approach to local studies. These terms once had precise meanings which can reveal much about the history of the landscape and illuminate important aspects of husbandry, stock farming, quarrying, wood management, communications and industry.

BALE HILLS

The minor place-name Bole Hill is very common in Derbyshire, wherever lead was once mined, and it serves to remind us of the places where the ore was burnt or smelted, long before smelt mills came into use. The 'bole' was a kind of open furnace, located on a ridge so as to take advantage of the prevailing wind. This is almost certainly how the ore was processed in the earliest phase of the Derbyshire industry and there are place-names and documents that take its history back to the twelfth century. On the other hand there are just two references to the

Backstone Beck, Ilkley. Backstones were large, flat mudstones on which oatcakes were baked. The *Oxford English Dictionary* (OED) has references to the word from 1531 but minor place-names take its history back to the twelfth century. The inference is that the stones were typically quarried in gills. (*Author's collection*)

word in the OED, and the first of these, dated 1670, tells us that this was how miners 'did fine their lead ... in ancient time'. David Hey has suggested that bole hills were no longer in use by 1580 and he is doubtless right but the practice may still have been fresh in the memory of men in the south Pennines. In 1587, for example, in a dispute that related to 'a place called Boalehill', a witness testified that the Earl of Shrewsbury 'had boals of lead' on the site and that 'he himself did burne dyvers boles of lead' there. The minor name survives in south Yorkshire as Bole Hill (Ecclesall), incorrectly explained as 'a smooth rounded hill' in *Place-Names of the West Riding of Yorkshire* (1961) but dealt with more accurately in *The Vocabulary of English Place-Names* (1997).

The late Mary Higham wrote a number of short articles on lead mining in Bowland and noted the use there of the same word. She quoted from the accounts of Henry de Lacy which included the expenses incurred in 1304–5 by mining operations at Ashnott. Two of the items that she listed related to the carriage of the ore to 'le boole' where it was burnt, and this use of the English word in a Latin text may indicate that the scribe had difficulty translating it. It appears to be the earliest example on record.

In lead-mining districts further to the north and east, Bale Hill is a place-name with exactly the same meaning and it doubtless represents a regional variation in pronunciation. Much of the evidence is in documents connected with Fountains Abbey, and their Memorandum Book contains an informative sequence of items for the period 1446–58. It describes Robert Merbeke as a 'baler' and records payments to him 'pro labore suo apud lez smeltes'. In an abbey lease of 1527 it was agreed that for every fother of lead they delivered to the monastery the tenants would receive in return 'at their foreseide bayll hylles eight lodes of ure'. In a Swaledale boundary dispute of *c*.1560, there was reference to land-holders cutting down wood that would then be burnt 'at their lead bales'. Several localities named Bale Hill survive in Nidderdale but when the minor names for Swaledale and Wensleydale have been collected others are likely to be found.

Almost incidentally this word suggests that surnames such as Boller, Boler, Boaler and Bowler need to be re-interpreted. The traditional explanation is that they are occupational in origin, for makers or sellers of bowls, but David Hey cast doubt on that when he referred to

Ralph le Bolere of Eyam (1300). The Derbyshire poll tax of 1381 has several examples in the lead-mining areas, e.g. Nicholas Boler of Tideswell, and these men or their ancestors seem certain to have been involved in smelting.

CALGARTH

Gardens are mentioned frequently in early title deeds but we know little about them. Stephen Moorhouse wrote an interesting piece on the topic in *West Yorkshire: an Archaeological Survey to A.D. 1500* (1981), making the point that most food was home grown in medieval society and that vegetables would have been a staple part of the diet in lower-class rural communities. One of the minor names that he discussed was 'leighton' or 'laughton' which had its origins in two Old English words that meant literally 'leek enclosure'. The leek, in all its varieties, was no doubt the dominant vegetable in those gardens but the term included other plants in the allium genus such as garlic and onions. The amount of starch in the medieval diet meant that herbs and spices assumed great importance, but 'leeks' were thought of as tasty in their own right and that may explain the importance of such specialist enclosures. The inference is that 'leighton' eventually developed the more general meaning of vegetable garden but its survival as a place-name is of real interest.

Teresa McLean listed cabbages, peas, beans, lentils, millet and onions as the basic vegetables of medieval England, but the common minor names Beanlands and Pease Close suggest that these vegetables would often have been grown in the fields rather than in plots close to the house. The cabbage, like the leek, appears to have been important enough to merit its own enclosure and it was an equally valuable part of the peasants' diet. It has given rise to very few place-names but Colworth (Bedfordshire) and Colwich (Staffordshire) derive from an Old English word for cabbage and are evidence of the plant's early importance.

In the north the generic term for brassica plants was kale and this occurs in the minor place-name Calgarth which means 'cabbage yard'. The spelling points to Scandinavian influence and references to the term date from the thirteenth century. Kail Hill in Appletreewick is from the same period and since it overlooks Calgarth House in Burnsall it is tempting to link the two place-names. This Calgarth was described as a 'culture' or 'close' in *c.*1280 but it was named

Calgarthouse in a fine of 1515 which indicates that by then it was a settlement site. One such 'cabbage yard' must have given rise to a by-name or surname, since a John Calgarth was named as the former tenant of a house in Markington in 1479.

Later examples of the word are also of interest, since they indicate how long the calgarth retained its importance. There were evidently such gardens well into the sixteenth century, for John Hudson was granted a lease in 1518 of 'one place in Esholte with the Call-garthe thereto belonginge'. The same property is listed in the Dissolution rental of 1540 as 'a house called the hole hall and the calle garth'. There are other clues as to how long it survived as a meaningful word: in 1575, for example, a Burton in Bishopdale inventory listed 'one calgarth spade' whilst in 1621 Edward Nealson of Abbotside willed that Jane Metcalfe should 'have houseroome and fire and one calgarth during her naturall life'. A lease of property in Askrigg in 1700 included 'one callgarth' and this too seems to have referred to a garden.

Calgarth: a 'culture' that was said to be in Appletreewick in 1303 but in Burnsall before the century was out. The farm sits in an ox-bow and the likelihood is that the Wharfe changed course in that period. Kail Hill is in the background. (*The author*)

The survival of Calgarth as a place-name makes it difficult to discover just when this specialised garden began to decline in importance, but a sequence of deeds for Horton in Ribblesdale may mark its transition into a place-name. In 1677, Lancelot Smithson conveyed a partitioned dwelling-house in the parish to Miles Taylor which included 'half the great calgarth or garden'. In 1693 this was described as a moiety of 'the Great Calgarth or garden on one side of Hebden farm' and in 1712 as 'half Hebden Call Garth'. Colegarth is a place-name with exactly the same meaning but with 'cole' rather than 'kale' as the prefix. This was the usual English spelling and it may sometimes have replaced the regional word. Colgarth Hill in Airton is one example, for it was spelt 'calgarthes' in 1603.

COMBS

The Celtic *cwm*, widely known because of the hymn *Cwm Rhondda*, was the word for a valley and it passed into the vocabulary of Old English with that meaning. It is listed in glossaries as *cumb* and we associate that element most strongly with south-west England. Nevertheless, there are similar place-names in several other parts of the country, especially in those areas where Britons and Anglo-Saxons were neighbours over a long period. In Cumberland, for example, it is a relatively frequent prefix, found in Cumcrook, Cumdivock and Cumwhitton, to mention just a few. One of the best-known Westmorland names is Great Coum in the Lake District, interpreted as the 'great valley'.

There is a group of place-names in the north-west corner of Yorkshire, particularly in areas close to Westmorland, which has received little attention but which may include some with *cumb* as an element. Among these are Comb (Sedbergh), Comb Gill (Garsdale), Combe (Dent), Comb Stoop (Buckden) and Combe Scar (Ingleton). Combs in Austwick and Comb Scar in Malham are not far away, and further east are Combes Hill (Appletreewick), Combs (Beamsley) and Combs near Ripon. Unfortunately, few early spellings of these names have been recorded.

In Malham, Comb Hill and Scar are said to derive from *camb* or *kambr*, the Old English and Old Norse words for a 'comb' or 'crest', the crest of a ridge that is. This meaning seems to be linked in some way with the cock's 'comb', a sort of modest northern equivalent of 'sierra', the Spanish word for a saw. Cam Fell in Horton in Ribblesdale and Cam Gill in Kettlewell seem certain to derive from that word. The interpretation of the Malham place-name is based on the topography and the earliest spelling located, i.e. Cam Scar, found in the 1849 tithe award. It is apt enough but the final interpretation may depend on the location of spellings much earlier than 1849.

Many more of the 'combs', notably those in Austwick, Dent and Sedbergh, were said in PNWR to derive from the Middle English word *culm*, which had meanings such as 'coal dust', 'peat dust' and 'soot'. Again, much of the evidence is late but a relatively early spelling for one of the Dent place-names supports that explanation, i.e. 'Cowlme'(1592). The first spellings for the other localities are: Lowcome in Sedbergh (1656); Coumerigg in Austwick (1676) and Cowme in Dent (1620). I have no doubt that the interpretation in these cases was influenced by spellings such as 'Cowme', which hint at a lost 'l' and by the fact that some of the names occur in places where there were or had been coal workings and smithies.

'Cowme' was certainly used in the north-west as a local word for peat dust, for Angus Winchester quotes a by-law of 1689 for Castlerigg in Cumberland which ordered tenants to clean up the 'cowme' when removing peats. The most frequently-quoted use of this word is the one found in George Owen's description of lime-kilns in Pembroke-shire, in which he referred to 'a fier of coales or rather culme, which is but the dust of coales' (1603). A Nottinghamshire document contains the Latin phrase 'carbonum marinorum et culmorum' (1348), a refer-ence that takes the word back to the fourteenth century at least.

Nevertheless, the evidence does not always point to 'culm' or to 'comb'. In the Teesdale village of Romaldkirk, for example, there is an early reference to a place-name that was not noted by Professor Smith. It is found in an undated grant of a vaccary and cannot be later than 1261. The grant included the right to enclose and assart land in 'Cumbis' or 'Coumbis', a name which seems likely to derive from the Celtic *cwm*. Similarly, Combs in Austwick has now been found on a map of 1619 as Combe Nabbe and here too the spelling may point away from the traditional interpretations. Only the location of earlier evidence will help to determine how many of these Pennine names contain the word for valley that predates 'gill' and 'dale'.

CRUTCHING

In the English Place-Name Society's ten volumes for Yorkshire there are just half a dozen places which have this element as a prefix and they are all in the Dales. It is a small number but others may turn up as more work is done on field-names. The spellings vary but they are sufficiently alike for us to feel that they share a common origin. Crutching Close features three times, in Langcliffe, Rylstone and Settle and there is Crutchon Close in Halton Gill; Crutchin Gill in Horton in Ribblesdale and Crutchenber Fell in Slaidburn. In each case the evidence is late, post 1840, collected from tithe awards and an Ordnance Survey map. Smith offered no etymology for the word and it was not listed in the section on 'elements' in volume VII of PNWR.

In the case of Crutchenber (Fell) it is possible to find much earlier spellings, using the work done on Slaidburn by C.J. Spencer and R.H. Postlethwaite. In the parish registers, for instance, there are half a dozen references between 1703 and 1810 to what was clearly a settlement, possibly a single dwelling. A succession of families had it as their place of residence, starting with Richard Coate 'de Crutchinbare' (1703) and ending with William Leach 'of Crutchinber' (1810). References from wills take the history back to the early seventeenth century when John Guy 'of Crutchanbarr' (1629) and Robert Scotson 'of Crutchonber in Bolland' (1615) were the occupiers of the property.

There is a further interesting reference in the Quarter Sessions records for 1719–20. Slaidburn was described there as consisting of three meers, named as Rishton Grange Meer, Hamerton Grange Meer and Essington Meer, all still recognisable territories. It was judged to be their common responsibility to maintain 'a cawsey which leads over Bolland Knotts' because it belonged 'equally amongst them being all within one township'. Soon afterwards they mentioned that 'a new cawsey over a place called Crutching bar' was being made. This seems to be a reference to the hill rather than to the settlement but it may indicate how the settlement name originated. In all these spellings the suffix clearly derives from a word for hill, either Old English *berg* or Old Norse *berg* – a very popular element in Ribblesdale.

The solution to the origin of 'Crutching' is to be found in the records of Fountains Abbey, specifically in those documents that inform us about livestock and customary practice among the tenants who were responsible for the abbey's cattle. There were numerous leases from 1512 onwards which had to do with the 'renewing' of the herds at twelve-month intervals; that is making arrangements for the older animals to be replaced by younger ones. Typically, 'nine of the oldest and most crochy cows' were passed on to the abbey's chief herdsman

The Cellarium, Fountains Abbey. Eight of the twenty-two bays were used to store provisions and they were formerly separated from the rest of the undercroft by a wall that has now been demolished.

early in the year and nine 'whyes' or heifers were introduced into the herd later. I have come across no other use of the adjective 'crochy', but the noun 'crochon' occurs regularly. It referred to the older beasts which were moved to good pasture land at Whitsuntide and fattened there in preparation for their slaughter in the autumn. An entry in the abbey rental of 1495–96, difficult to translate accurately, seems to link such a pasture with 'lez Crochons'. These early details of a long-forgotten custom demonstrate just how an enclosure or grazing ground might acquire the type of place-name mentioned earlier.

That is not quite the end of the matter, for in a published account book for the abbey, which covered the years from 1446 to 1459, there are several items which seem certain to refer to crochons, where the word has been mistakenly transcribed as 'crochous'. In more than one case it is found in a list of specialist words for cattle such as drapes (milkless cows) and stirkettes (young bullocks), so it is reasonable to assume that an error was made. The editor of the accounts judged that 'crochous' was a place-name and it was duly included in Smith's volumes on the West Riding.

DUB

Until recently the dialect word 'dub' was in fairly general use in the northern counties and it is probably still known in some communities. Although the etymology is obscure it means a puddle or a pool and can be found in Scottish texts from the early 1500s. A correspondent some years ago told me that during his childhood in the Leeds area it was regularly used to mean a puddle of rainwater: it was also used jokingly to describe much bigger stretches of water, and emigrants from Swaledale to America, writing home in the early 1800s, are said to have called the Atlantic ocean the 'gert dub'.

In certain contexts, deep pools in rivers or streams were also called 'dubs', and these are said to have been used as places to wash sheep. Angus Winchester links them with specially-built washfolds where the sheep would be gathered before being forced into the water. A Nidderdale boundary description of 1481 refers to 'le Frier dubb' in Thornton Beck, and this may have been such a location, a place where sheep belonging to Fountains Abbey were washed. A lease of 1514 described the tenant's obligation to wash and clip the sheep as a customary practice, and it is easy to see how traditional wash pits of this kind could give rise to minor place-names. Some of those found in the Dales can no doubt be explained in that way.

One of the most interesting place-names in this group is found in depositions relating to a dispute in Swaledale in *c*.1560. It had to do with a beck that divided Marrick and Marske, called Bradhow Beck in the depositions, and one witness claimed that he had seen Marrick men fishing on both sides of the stream. He also said that he knew very well 'the damme callide Marrige stelling dubbe' at the head of the beck, and the inference is that this was a traditional fishery. Somewhat later than this date, 'dubs' were described as deep pools where fish congregated in summer, or when the river was low; 'stell' and 'stelling' are north-country words which could refer either to fishing sites or animal enclosures, but the context here makes it clear that 'Marrige stelling dubbe' was a fishery. The dam or weir mentioned by the witnesses was an essential feature of such fisheries. The site is doubtless remembered in the place-names Lower Stelling Farm and Stelling Road.

There are large numbers of place-names in north-west Yorkshire with 'dub' as either a suffix or prefix, and similar names are found in Westmorland and Cumberland. Unfortunately, much of the evidence is again quite late, first recorded in tithe awards or on Ordnance Survey maps. Typical of these late names are Dubbs (Arncliffe), Dubbs Lane (Buckden), Dubs Beck (Rathmell), Dub Laithe (Burnsall) and Dub Hole (Litton). More unusual are Sweethill Dub and Broats Dub, both in Sedbergh. Names for which earlier evidence has been noted are Dub in Austwick (1771), Dubb Green in Bowland (1652), Cow Dub in Dent (1621) and Dub Garth in Clapham (1600). Dub Cote in Horton in Ribblesdale was where one branch of the Howson family lived from before 1548, and the original dwelling may have been the 'cote' that survives in the place-name.

I suspect that many of these names had no connection with either fishing or sheep washes, for local records show that 'dub' was often used in a quite different way. For example, the Airton court roll of 1611 refers to 'a rating dubb in the syke' made by Christopher Preston, and exactly the same term is used in a Kilnsey deed of 1636. These were pools in which hemp or flax was soaked, and they were created by damming the stream or possibly diverting water from the stream into a hollow. 'Rating' was part of a process that separated the fibres from the stem of the plant, and the Yorkshire word had exactly the same meaning as the English 'ret'. It was in common use in the seventeenth century when numerous houses had their own 'dub' or pit. A house leased in Hanlith in 1673 had 'one hempe dub thereunto belonging' and one in Malham, in 1600, had 'one hempe pitt for to rayt hempe in'.

This was not an industry. The flax and hemp were required by householders for their own use, to make linen and coarser fabrics. In 1617, the inventory for Cams House in Aysgarth included 'two lining hand towells and 4 cowrse ones', along with heckles that would have been used by the housewife to comb the fibres. It is difficult to determine just how long this rural practice lasted, and little appears to have been written about it, but much of the place-name evidence goes back only to *c*.1600. No doubt it declined as the factory industry developed: one Malham man could remember seeing the ruined pits in his younger days, early in the 1800s.

HIPPINGS

In the Dales, and other parts of the north of England, 'hippings' or hipping stones was once the usual term for stepping stones across a river. It was the antiquarian Ralph Thoresby who first felt that he needed to explain what hippings were, having written about 'the hippings in the brook' that divided Batley and Leeds. He defined them as 'large stones set in a shallow water at a step's distance from each other, to pass over by'. Earlier, in a letter dated 1703, he had written something very similar and it is this reference that is offered by the OED as the first mention of the word. The likelihood is, though, that the term has a much longer history, since the verb 'to hip', meaning to hop, can be traced back to *c*.1300.

A very early reference occurs in a charter for Beamsley, dated from before 1219: it mentions a place called 'Hoppondstanes' and this seems likely to be an early version of hippings. The inhabitants of Erringden, in the Calder valley, were accused in 1609 of not mending 'the

The stepping-stones or 'hippings' at Bolton Priory. Their early history is uncertain but they have long provided direct access to the parish church for the townships on the east side of the river. (*Author's collection*)

hoppengstones betwixt Stobyng and Mythom', which is probably the source of the Mytholmroyd place-name Hippens End, first noted in 1758. Similar minor place-names exist in numerous townships, referring either to the stepping stones themselves or to minor features associated with them. Typical examples are Nappa Hippings, Green Hippins in Wigglesworth and Hippings Lane in Burnsall. Wenning Hippins, in Clapham, were said in 1698 to be in 'the King's high road between London and Kendal' and the locality is mentioned in the parish registers from 1639. The Arncliffe registers record the drowning of a girl at 'Buckden hippins' in 1676.

A reference in 1707 to 'Gisburn hippings bridge' is more unusual and it illustrates the way in which 'hippings' was emerging as a place-name element. In fact there are very few early references in local records to stepping stones, and I have found no mention of hipping stones before the seventeenth century, so it may be that they came into greater prominence after 1555, when an Act of Parliament made local communities responsible for their highways.

The extent to which that might become a cause for dispute emerges in a Quarter Sessions case of 1657 between the inhabitants of Yeadon and Rawdon on the one hand and Mr Calverley on the other. The townsmen claimed that they shared a right of way to Calverley 'over certayne great stones or hippings laid, sett and placed in and thorough the river of Ayre and … thorough one close of land … called the hipping close'. This piece of land was on the Calverley side of the river and belonged to Walter Calverley whose workmen, it was said, 'did cleave, break in sunder and digg upp' the stones. The aggrieved townsmen added colour to their story when they described the workmen's implements as 'great malles, gavelackes, spades, hacks and iron wedges'. The Rawdon tithe award of 1840 has 'Hipping Stones' as a minor place-name, and the 'Hipperstone Ing' of the Calverley award is no doubt the close of land where that unneighbourly act took place.

LODGE

The Normans brought this word with them, and the OED gives more than a dozen related meanings, most of them connected with a small dwelling in temporary or seasonal use. Specialised buildings were the masons' lodge and the park-keeper's lodge and the second of these certainly gave rise to a number of minor place-names. Nevertheless, not one of the meanings in the dictionary fully explains how the word developed in the Dales, either as a place-name or a surname.

It has a long history there for it features in a Fountains Abbey charter of 1190–99, albeit in Latin: 'Item grangias de Aldeburg, Birnebem, Dacram et Burthweith, et logias Beuerley, scilicet, Popelton, Sixford, etc'. The surname Lodge appears to have been occupational in origin: an early fourteenth-century memorandum from the Coucher Book of Kirkstall Abbey refers to a lodge for herdsmen in Bowland (unum loghe pro pastoribus) which was in the care of a man named 'Willelmus del Loghe, custos' – a lodge-keeper. By the fourteenth century the name was well established and there were families called 'de Loge' or 'de Loege' in Buckden, Rimington and Kirkby Malzeard, probably unrelated.

These abbey lodges may have started out as temporary shelters for herdsmen but the term developed a more specialised meaning as stock-keeping increased in importance and they were almost certainly permanent settlements by the 1300s: some of them, Darnbrook and

Cow Gill Cote. The door and windows remind us that this uninhabited building was once a lodge of Fountains Abbey. It features in the abbey's accounts from the mid-1400s when a wether flock was kept there. (*The author*)

Hardcastle for example, gave rise to surnames in that period. In the Fountains Abbey lease book 'lodge' was used as a synonym for 'dairy house' or 'fee house' by the sixteenth century; that is an establishment largely given over to raising cattle and providing dairy produce. The fact that Nutwithcote was called a 'graunge or loge' in 1495 indicates how far it had moved away from the idea of a shepherd's hut. The entry for Sigsworth in the rental for that year provides us with a clearer picture of what a lodge was:

> John Thakwrey ... holds ... the lodge of Syxford, for which he keeps 40 cows and one bull of the stock of the monastery at all times of the year, and renders annually from the profits of the said cows 20 stone 8 pounds of butter, worth 12d a stone; 53 stone 4 pounds of cheese, worth 8d a stone, and 20 stirks at Whitsun, worth 4s each ... and lastly he pays 13s 4d annually from his farm, in equal portions at the said terms.   Sum £7 15s 6¼d.

By that time the tenants who occupied these farms were described as 'lodgers' or 'logiers'. In 1509, for example, Thomas Atkinson had the lease of Haddockstones where he had a herd of sixty cows: he undertook 'to delyver his butter and chesse yerlye to the cheshous in Fountaynes ... as appeerteneth for so many kye, after the custome usid and had emongs the loigers in Nidredaill'. It is difficult to say whether the men called 'de Loge' in the fourteenth century would have had similar obligations.

The changes that came about after the Dissolution marked the end of the traditional lodges but they were not immediately forgotten. In a tithe case of 1579, quoted by Whitaker, William Anderson testified that he was familiar with the lands that Fountains Abbey had owned on Malham Moor having been a herdsman there twenty years before the Dissolution: he 'dwelt together with thre more shepeheardes at a lodge in Fountance Fell'. Perhaps the older meaning of a small or temporary shelter had never been lost: in 1607 there was reference to a 'callfe lodge' on Hanlith Moor.

RAKE

This is a common minor name in its own right and it is also found in numerous compounds. In the former category are The Rake in Clapham and The Rakes in Appletreewick whilst Hartlington Rakes and Hebden Rakes are typical two-theme names. In a few compound names 'rake' is the prefix, e.g. Rakes Bottom (Threshfield), Rakes Wood (Buckden) and Rake Ford (Sedbergh). One of the best known of all these names, certainly to the outsider, is Prior Rakes in Malham.

In *Malham and Malham Moor* (1971) Arthur Raistrick commented on the popularity of 'rake' and expressed the opinion that it was a dialect word of Scandinavian origin and 'applied to the steep portion of a road'. It is true that it sometimes refers to a track, especially to a narrow path on a hillside, and in the Lake District this may be the usual meaning. Diana Whaley said recently that all seven of the examples that she had noted in Cumbria described 'spectacularly rugged routes'. Among those she quoted were Lord's Rake in Eskdale and Lady's Rake in Borrowdale. The earliest reference that she had found was for Rakefoot (St John's) in 1597. It was her view that the word is of uncertain etymology.

Angus Winchester discussed the term in connection with 'drift ways'; that is the rights of way on to the fells for sheep and cattle. Significantly, he stated that 'rake' was used both for a way that led on to the hill side and also for the grazing ground itself: there was clearly a close relationship between the two meanings. In particular he quoted a document of 1654 in which the word 'outrake' was used: initially this may have identified the path used by the cattle on to the mountain but in the document concerned it described a place on Langdale Pikes called Tentters and White Cragg 'from the low to the height'.

Bolton Priory records provide us with much earlier material: in 1310–14 payments were made for assarting and digging ditches 'in le Rakes' at Halton, and this must surely refer to new clearances, as parts of the waste were converted into farm land. The 'rakes' would therefore have been a reference to common pasture, probably moorland. Later references are certainly to pasture: in 1536, for example, Richard Atkinson of Pott near Masham, a Fountains Abbey tenant, paid an out-rent for 'a cow pasture named the Cowe Rake' – exactly the same rent that the tenants had paid in 1495–96. In 1520, John Buck of Darnbrook bound himself to keep a flock of wethers on the 'raykkes' as he customarily had done. Flock Rake was listed by Smith as a place-name on Malham Moor and this occurs earlier as a word in Hanlith, i.e. 'all that flockraike or sheep pastures' (1664).

It is not always clear exactly what the pasturage rights were and how they were apportioned. In some cases it is certain that a 'rake' was

The Dry Valley, properly named Watlowes. In 1569 Prior Rakes was said to lie 'betwixt the watter of Gordell ... and the watter of Malhme descendinge from Malhme Watter Terne ... down a gill called Watlows'. The dry stone wall marks the boundary between the estates of Bolton Priory and Fountains Abbey. (*The author*)

not just a stretch of common grazing but a stinted pasture; that is an enclosed area in which a number of farmers enjoyed historic rights: these appear to have been determined originally by their ancestors' land holdings. The individual farmer's allotments were known as gates, usually beast gates or sheep gates. In this sense 'gate' was the right for an animal to 'go' on to the pasture. A tithe dispute of 1598 concerned itself with pasture rights on Fountains Fell, debating whether the dissolved monastery kept it in their own possession or whether the tenants of the farms on Malham Moor 'had stint and rake of goodes' there.

A sequence of deeds for Hanlith in Malhamdale illustrates another of the related meanings that the word could have: 'winter raike' in 1629 was later defined as 'winter stint', and in 1674 this was explicitly 'part of the edige and winter raike within the open fields of Hanleith'. In this case the rake or right to pasturage was in the town's arable land during the dead time of winter. There appears to have been no residual sense of 'path' in this meaning although a 'rake' could refer to a path in other parts of the Pennines: in Rawdon, in 1564, a tenant referred to 'the sheppe raikes or paithes' on the moor.

Prior Rakes in Malham owes its name to the association with Bolton Priory and, although we know little about its earliest history, the nature of the terrain indicates that it was pasture. Perhaps it stabilised as a place-name only after the Dissolution although it would have been a descriptive phrase long before that: it was referred to in 1606 as 'the enclosed ground called New Close or Prior Rake'. Raistrick quoted this deed, and his summary of the contents establishes that it was by then a stinted pasture, divided into one hundred and seven parts, with four parts accorded to every oxgang and one part to every toft. As early as 1569 a dispute had taken place about the 'raike ... pertenynge to the ... tenants and freeholders of the east side of the towne of Malhame called the Priour Raike'.

So familiar was the word in the sense of pasture that it was occasionally employed as a verb: in 1676, a Hanlith tenant called Richard Wiggan had rights for his animals in several pasture grounds including both Prior Rakes and the Weets. These granted him 'sufficient herbage and feeding for the said beasts to raike, feed and depasture' there. In 1617 an Oakworth document refers to the fear that cattle might 'rake over' into an area of disputed pasture.

STONERY

I find no mention of this word in the OED or in specialised glossaries but it occurs in both Wharfedale and Airedale in contexts that inform us about a long-forgotten practice. In 1619, for example, a lease to Reginald Heber of Flasby reserved the 'stonearies' and coal mines to the use of the lord but did not make clear exactly what a stonery was. A later lease, in 1685, allowed Michael Hudson of Austby the right to exploit the 'quarries of stone and stonaries' and this at least is evidence that the stonery was not simply a quarry.

The chance survival of a bundle of old deeds for Addingham has solved the problem. One document of 1629 refers to a grant to Francis Hodgson of Nesfield of 'all that stonerye of Lymestone ... on the weste side of the River of Wharffe', in a close called Smithy Greaves. We learn later that 'the same stonerye' had been 'of lait Lymitted, staked, sett forth or devided' from the rest of Smithy Greaves, presumably so that Francis Hodgson's activities would be confined to that area. The lease required him to 'make a good and sufficient fence of Stoupes and Rayles all alonge after the west side of the Stonerye'.

It is a reference to the stonery as a 'Lymestonbedd' that tells us what Francis Hodgson was doing, for limestone is not the underlying rock in that part of the valley, although limestone boulders were found in the glacial deposits there. Effectively, the stonery was the location of these boulders in quantities that made their extraction a profitable enterprise. An almost contemporary lease granted several men in Draughton 'full and free liberty to dig and get Lymestone' from named closes in the township and the right 'to lead and carrye awaye the same'. Even more explicitly a tenant in Bingley was given authority in 1620 'to dig ... for limestones and to burn, sell and dispose of them'.

Local historians have long been aware of Bingley's role in this local industry and there is an evocative petition in the rolls of the Quarter Sessions, dated 1699, that links it to social problems in the township. Part of the document is worth quoting for the picture it paints of the effect that the stoneries had on the landscape:

> For a long tyme there have been and now are, great quantities of Lyme Stones gotten promiscuously in Bingley and Micklethwaite ... by means whereof the ground is digged upp and very much impaired, to the great decay of the yearly value of the same.

The site of Clapham Tarn. There was formerly a tarn to the south-west of the Norber Erratics and the site is now marked by a decayed ring wall and reddish-brown vegetation. The minor place-name Tarn Thwaite confirms the location.
(*Peter Van Demark*)

The petition refers to the getting of limestone over a long period, which is hardly specific, but Whitaker quotes from a building account of 1437 when bushels of lime were purchased in Addingham for work that was being carried out on Skipton Castle. The leases which mention the practice all date from the early 1600s so it may be that this was when the industry was becoming more organised. The sequence of Addingham deeds also helps to chart its decline for the old liberties no longer applied by 1790 and the tenant of Smithy Greaves had the right only to gather lime-stones out of the river for his personal use.

TEIND

The OED entry for 'tithe' makes the point that its linguistic history is shared with the word 'tenth' and that the spelling was retained because of the special meaning that it developed, that is as the tenth part of produce that was pledged to the support of a priest. In the north 'teind' was a collateral form and it is found frequently in early Yorkshire documents. Typical references are to 'forgetyn tendes' (1444) and 'teande hay' (1573).

In combination with the regional word 'lathe' it identified what we now refer to as the tithe barn, a term which was rare in the county until quite recently. The earliest reference that I have come across is in the by-name John Tendlathe, a Leeds tax payer in 1379. It next occurs in a sequence of title deeds to property in Askwith: in 1426 John Wayte of Askwith quitclaimed his rights in land that was described as lying between a barn called 'Teyndlath' on the east and a 'garth' or garden on the west. This deed was in Latin and it seems likely that the clerk inserted the local word to make the meaning absolutely clear. With the spelling 'teen lathe' the term was later included in the *Craven Glossary* (1828).

I have no doubt that this word explains a number of minor place-names in the Dales. The connection was noted by Smith in his comment on the field-name Teenley Croft in Horton in Ribblesdale which he linked with 'teenlayth', a spelling that is used in a deposition dated 1693. He saw it as distinct from 'Tyethe laethe Croft', mentioned in a deed of 1588, which he attributed to Titla Barn in the same parish. It is a development that can be traced to the colloquial pronunciation of 'lathe'.

It was quite usual for dialect speakers not to pronounce the final 'th' in words and place-names, and the practice resulted in some confused spellings, even among the clerks. In 1533, for example, John Midgley made provision in his will for Agnes Garthfor – a double misspelling of Garforth. We should therefore consider that 'teen lathe' lies behind a number of other poorly-documented minor names such as Tenley in Hellifield and Teenley Hill in Wigglesworth.

Chapter 2

Places and People

Although the etymology of place-names can tell us a great deal about matters such as clearance, settlement, farming practices and the landscape itself, it can be valuable to take the study one step further and link a place-name with a particular family, a house or a significant episode in history, locally or nationally. Such stories can capture a passing moment or relate an unfolding sequence of events but either way they provide us with revealing insights into aspects of social and religious history. Where a document contains a single item of interest it may serve to point us in the direction of additional material that allows us to build up a fuller picture. Such information must be sought in a wide variety of records, and the place-name serves as a link to the references.

COSH – A MOMENT IN THE HISTORY OF A PENNINE FARM

If we follow the river Skirfare to its source we pass through a series of picturesque villages and hamlets whose names become a sort of walkers' litany: Arncliffe, Litton, Halton Gill, Foxup and, finally, Cosh. This tiny settlement, some 450 metres above sea level, was always remote: when an old farmer was reminiscing about life at Cosh in the early 1900s, he remembered how he used to set out for Settle with his horse and cart once every month, in order to stock up on provisions. At its peak there were three houses in the hamlet, a small and almost self-sufficient community. However, this has always been marginal land and nobody lives permanently at Cosh now.

We first encounter the place-name in the records of Fountains Abbey, where it is referred to as Greenfield Cosh, implying that its original links were with Green Field at the head of Langstrothdale. The early spellings of Green Field show quite clearly that it meant the green fell or mountain. The etymology of Cosh is less obvious but in the fifteenth century a 'cosh' appears to have been a small cottage or hut, possibly a more pejorative term than 'cote', and this suggests how unimportant the early settlement may have been. It is interesting therefore to note occasional early references to the place-name Greenfield Cote, possibly the same dwelling.

We know little about the farm at Cosh over the centuries, except for the names of its owners, the families who lived there, and the rents they paid. In 1495–96, for example, when it belonged to Fountains Abbey, Thomas Langstroghe and Ralph Metcalfe were the tenants, each man paying 20s per annum for his share of the lease. This was exactly the same valuation that had been recorded fifty years earlier and it would be recorded again at the time of the Dissolution. The inference may be that little changed at Cosh over the centuries but, fortunately, details of one small incident have survived in the records of the Quarter Sessions, bringing some colour to the hamlet's history. It is a sheep-stealing allegation that concerned a farmer called Lancelot Metcalfe, possibly a descendant of the Dissolution tenant. The circumstances make us smile, even though the matter may have had serious consequences.

John Londsbrooke, the constable for Litton, was the person who brought the matter to the attention of the magistrates in October 1675. He recounted how he had made a search at Cosh, almost certainly 'upon information received' from Lancelot's neighbour, Thomas Proctor. Lancelot Metcalfe answered Londsbrooke's knock at the door, appearing with 'noe close [clothes] upon him but his shirt': when he saw the constable he fled and could not be apprehended on that occasion. According to the constable there were several cuts of mutton in the cottage, including two whole hinder quarters and two breasts, none of these 'cutt or parted in sunder'. More seriously there were also two shoulders of mutton, and part of this had been cut: in fact it was boiling in a pan on the fire. On further search the skin of the sheep was discovered 'on the hey moure [high moor], in an outhouse in the field'.

Lancelot was finally arrested, having been located in an outbuilding, hiding under a hay mow. The examination carried out by Mr Cuthbert Wade sought to establish whether the sheep could have belonged to Metcalfe. He was asked how many sheep he wintered at Cosh and if they were all still alive. He replied 'onelie three ewes which had each of them a lambe' and, as far as he knew, they were all still alive. Nor had he bought any sheep in the spring or summer. How then, pursued

Mr Wade, had he come by the mutton found in his house and why had he run away when he saw the constable at his door? Strange to relate Lancelot Metcalfe had no idea 'how they came theire' and he had hidden himself because he was afraid of the constable, knowing that he had taken out a warrant for his arrest. He did not say why he had started boiling the mutton when he knew that he was suspected of stealing two sheep, but perhaps he thought he might somehow eat the evidence before the constable had time to act on the warrant.

FORNAH GILL CLOSE

One chapter in the history of this minor place-name emerges in a series of depositions that relate to a tithe case of 1598. These have survived among the records of the Consistory Court of the Archbishop of York and are in English, taking us back to before the Dissolution, in some cases twenty or thirty years earlier. The parties in the dispute were Edward Talbott, the farmer of the Rectory of Kirkby Malham, and Thomas Proctor, although the real interest in the documents lies more in the incidental information that we are offered by the witnesses than in the outcome of the dispute. Many of those who gave evidence were former tenants or servants of Fountains Abbey and several of them were in their late eighties.

It is significant that when Thomas Proctor used the place-name he referred to it as 'Fornagill Close', the form preferred by the clerks in the interrogatories for the trial, whereas the witnesses remembered the pre-enclosure names, Fornagill pasture or Fornagill ground. In fact one of the court's concerns was the timing of the enclosure of Fornah Gill, and they pressed for details of how the same 'was boundred or lymitted'. In particular it was important for them to establish 'whether the pastures ... called Fornagill ... at the tyme of the dissolucion ... and before and sence, were common or inclosed groundes ... and when and about what tyme were the same inclosed'.

The evidence on that point is very revealing: Roger Buck, aged seventy-six, testified that in 1598 the pasture was 'devided from other groundes ... with walls and other fences, and ... inclosid on all sides saving at the topp' where it lay open to Fountains Fell. John Lawson of Arncliffe had known the area for more than seventy-two years and could also remember that Fountains Fell formerly adjoined 'the ground called Fornagill ... lying open to it', that is without walls.

Penyghent from Fountains Fell. It is first referred to in a document of 1307, as a boundary marker 'between the fees of John de Moubray and Henry de Percy'. It incorporates the Old Welsh 'penn' meaning a hill. (*The author*)

There may have been no walls in that pre-Dissolution period but the herdsmen knew exactly the limits of each of the adjoining properties. John Lawson and others could reel them off with great familiarity, clearly aware of exactly where Fornah Gill lay in relation to Fountains Fell, Westside House, Neals Ing and Sleights. These men, to use their own term, had 'looked to' the sheep in all kinds of weather over many years and they knew every nook and cranny of the moors.

Nor had old age dimmed the memories they had of the customs and traditions that marked the pasture's function and history. Francis Benson recalled that Fornagill pasture was 'an high, moorishe and mossy ground, fitt onely for someringe and not for wynteringe of any cattell'; he also remembered that 'the herdemen were boorded in the somer tymes att one Richard Fenwicke's houses at Penny Gent'. This 'summering' extended from St Ellen Day to Michaelmas, and Richard Knowles told how he and other herdsmen had driven the animals to and from the abbey each year, almost twenty miles away. William Lambert, aged ninety, was one of several men with clear memories of

Kilnsey – an important centre for Fountains Abbey. On the right is Kilnsey Hall, the home of the Wade family in the seventeenth century, now restored. The house is known to have been uninhabited in 1878 and it served later as a barn. One writer described it as 'ruinous' in 1980. (*The author*)

taking the abbey's sheep to Kilnsey to be clipped, 'opon the morrow after Midsummer day ... the woll whollie caried away to the Abby'. John Lawson commented on the fact that the cattle and sheep carried 'the burne and mark of the Abbey'.

Sheep were not the only animals on the pasture, or 'goods' if we are to use the herdsmen's term. On one occasion there were also ten 'kyne' and a bull, two mares and their followers, and a riding nag, 'all in the same ground feding and lying'. The stories that eighty-year-old Ralph Buck of Darnbrook could tell must have taken the oral history of Fornah Gill back into the late 1400s for as a boy he had known and talked to the abbey's herdsmen on the moor. His memories emphasise the difficult and solitary nature of their occupation, and he was able also to paint a vivid picture of the dangers they could encounter. He spoke of having seen 'the heardes milke the Abbei's kyne in the same ground, lying ther swords and bucklers besides them whilest they were milking'. That was presumably because the Scots were still likely to make raids south at that time.

Part of the problem for the court was to understand the ways in which farming practices could differ before and after the Dissolution. A family called Sedgwick held the lease of Fornah Gill from the late 1400s at least and they were required to keep a wether flock belonging to the abbey on the pasture. They kept their own flocks on the same commons but there is evidence to suggest that the abbey's animals might be wintered at Dacre in Nidderdale or at Fornah Gill House. In the 1550s, though, the Sedgwicks had their sheep on the pasture through the summer and 'in Winter tyme also if the wether [weather] did serve'. The family also had gist cattle on Fornagill Close after the Dissolution. This change in the status of pastures in the Dales marks a watershed in the region's history and farming practices.

FRIARS HEAD

The house of this name is in Gargrave parish, beautifully situated on rising ground, less than a mile to the south of Winterburn. The imposing façade has four projecting gables which rise to the full height of the building and are adorned with finials. One of the first writers to comment on Friars Head was the architectural historian Louis Ambler who described it as 'a stately house' built by the Proctor family. He compared the distinctive windows in the upper part of the gables with those in one or two halls in Lancashire, whilst Nikolaus Pevsner drew attention to their similarity with windows in Kildwick Hall, some ten miles distant: he described the building as 'unusually good'. Marie Hartley and Joan Ingilby came upon the house 'with a shock of delighted surprise'. There can be few more attractive houses in the Dales.

Although it is generally agreed that Friars Head was built in the 1600s, nobody has ventured to say exactly when. Only Ambler dared to be more precise, saying it was 'early seventeenth century'. It must in any case have replaced a much earlier house, since there are references to the place-name in deeds and wills from *c*.1500. In 1507, for example, Thomas Proctor made his will and left 'Frerehead' to his wife Eden and their son Stephen: in 1517 Roger Proctor of Cowper Cote asked his kinsman Stephen Procter of 'Frerhede' to be responsible for the tuition of his daughters Isabel and Mabel. The Proctor family was later to claim that the tenancy had been in their hands since the mid 1300s.

Much of Winterburn was held by Furness Abbey through that period, and the previous house is listed in a pre-Dissolution rental as 'Freerhed', valued at £8 3s 4d. Other named properties were Winterburn Hall, Cowper Cote, Newfield and Cowhouse, and their combined rents totalled £22 10s 0d. 'Winterburn Town' was valued at £11 10s 0d, and properties in Eshton, Flasby and Airton at £9 9s 0d. The fact that the Proctors of Friars Head acted as bailiffs for the abbey and were responsible for collecting those sums of money may help to explain the meaning of the place-name. Professor Smith has suggested that it might refer to a nearby hill, one 'resembling a friar's head', but a more likely explanation is that 'friar' points to a link with the monks of Furness, for it is a common element in Yorkshire place-names that had monastic links. The location of the house is likely to account for the suffix 'head', for it lies above the flat lands alongside Winterburn Beck.

The Proctor family is known to have had a long association with Furness Abbey, and the name John Proketour is found in their records as early as 1356. The surname may already have been hereditary, for a second John Proktur was taxed in 1379 at Clapham where Furness also had property. It is a shortened form of 'procurator' which was a term used for an agent or steward, and the Proctors were therefore important employees of the abbey. In view of the offices that the family held in the Dales, right up to the Dissolution, it seems possible that they had acted for the abbey over many generations. There can be no doubt that they prospered until the abbey was dissolved, and Friars Head may have been in their possession throughout that period. The claim they were to make in 1557 of a link going back 200 years is therefore quite credible.

The Dissolution inevitably brought about changes for those who held abbey property but the tenants at Winterburn had their lives completely disrupted in the years leading up to that event. We are made aware of that in the depositions made by several members of the Proctor family in cases brought to the Court of Star Chamber in the 1530s. They accused the abbey's steward, Lord Clifford of Skipton Castle, of sending his men to oust them from their property, and

Friars Head, Winterburn, a property in the possession of Furness Abbey until the Dissolution. The abbey acquired the estate from the Graindorge family of Flasby in the second half of the twelfth century. (*The author*)

the Proctors' petition paints a dramatic picture. John Proctor named several local men in a group of eight persons who:

> riotously and with force entred yn to the premises, and dyd expelle your sayd subjecte, and his pottes, pannys, plat or dishes … and oder stuffe of household to the value of xxli [£20] did take and caste oute of the same house yn the height street, wherof a grett part was takyn and carried away by the same … and the oxen, kyen and other yong bestes of your sayd subjecte then pasturyng on the premysses they dyd take, chace and dryve awaye att places unknawyn … they dyd also take your sayd subjecte thens untyll the castell of Skypton and … dyde imprison your subjecte by the space of too monethes …

Gabriel and Thomas Proctor, together with a tenant named Thomas Halton, actually made accusations against the Earl of Cumberland himself, blaming him for similar offences and saying that his claim to the property was a forgery, the work of a monk named Hugh Brown. This man had, they said, broken into a chest in the monastery which contained blank indentures and the convent seal, and used these to manufacture a lease for the Earl which granted him the Winterburn lands on very favourable terms. According to Morkill the Proctors won their case but had still not regained control of their lands over twenty years later. In the petition of 1557 that was referred to earlier, Gabriel Proctor stated that he and 'hys ancessowres called Proctours successyfely one after another … haythe hade ye sayd manore by lease more than tow hunderethe yere' but were now 'clerely beggered'.

Thomas Proctor of Friars Head was a colourful character and a very intelligent man. He had interests in farming, the construction of canals

Furness Abbey, the entrance to the Chapter House, 1845. Originally an important Savignac foundation, it was incorporated into the powerful Cistercian Order in 1147. Its estates included property in Craven and the region around Ingleborough and Whernside. At the Dissolution it was second only to Fountains in wealth.
(*Author's collection*)

and roads, and especially in mining, and he spent much of his life seeking to revolutionise the making of iron, using fuels other than charcoal. He obtained a patent in 1589, on such favourable terms that he would have become a very rich man if his experiments had been successful. Unfortunately, he was not a good businessman and because he was sometimes less than honest he let down both business partners and friends. He had sold the lease of Friars Head to the Dowager Countess of Cumberland in 1574, and purchased an estate at Warsill which had previously belonged to Fountains Abbey. Even this property later passed out of his control. Despite his many talents and a fertile imagination, he seems never to have made the most of his abilities.

He is less well known than his son Stephen who was born at Friars Head in 1562 and later knighted. A fine of 1596–97 records Stephen's purchase of the Fountains Abbey estate from William and Thomas Gresham, and he built Fountains Hall about 1611 with stone taken from the abbey. He also created for himself an apparently fictitious ancestry which is commemorated in the windows of the hall. By all accounts he was not a well-loved man and comments on his character include such pejorative words as 'unscrupulous' and 'ruthless': J.R. Walbran wrote of him that 'after a life of ambitious speculation, pursued with so little rectitude of conduct as to have been visited by legal punishment and parliamentary censure', he sank deeper and deeper into debt and was dead by 1619, outlived by his father Thomas.

Fountains Hall may stand as a testimony to the grand ambition of Stephen Proctor but the present Friars Head is unlikely to have any direct connection with the family. We cannot yet be certain just when it was built, nor by whom, but we should perhaps consider the possibility that it was the work of the Listers of Thornton in Craven. The lease had passed to the Countess of Cumberland in 1574 but eight years later William Lister of Thornton mentioned the house in his will. Among many bequests was 'the lease of the Frearhead' which he had acquired from his 'cousin Marton' and which in turn he bequeathed to members of his family. His daughter Ellen was to hold it for seven years, in order to 'preferre her in mariage' after which time it would go to her brother Michael. Michael was certainly in residence in the early 1600s and he died at Friars Head in 1618.

Fountains Hall (detail), built *c.*1611 by Stephen Proctor using stone from the abbey. Pevsner compared it with Hardwick in Derbyshire and described the centre part as 'of uncommon ingenuity and interest'. (*Peter Van Demark*)

NEALS ING

Neals Ing is in Stainforth township, in a remote location at the head of Tongue Gill. Just to the north-west lies the former lodge of Fornah Gill House, now the site of a barn, and Sannet Hall is roughly the same distance to the south-west. It was the home of a family named Frankland in the early 1500s and they were the tenants until 1620, when Richard Frankland conveyed his lease to John Tennant of Starbotton. Actually the D'Arcy family owned Neals Ing at that time but Sir Edward D'Arcy sold it to Richard Horsfall of Storthes Hall in 1652. It then passed via his grandson to the Dawsons of Langcliffe and they still had it in their possession at the end of the nineteenth century. When Pudsay Dawson granted a seven-year lease of Neals Ing to John Holgate in 1792 it was part of an estate that also included Fornah Gill and almost 100 acres of land.

Usually there is little that is exciting in the simple story of owners and tenants but life at Neals Ing could be eventful. The farm is mentioned in 1572, for example, when Thomas Frankland was accused of 'killing and destroying deere' on the neighbouring fells. A similar episode, in 1544, involved up to a score of armed men who assaulted a keeper and terrified the local population. Thomas Frankland's offence saw him imprisoned for some time in Skipton Castle, but he did not stay there very long. Neals Ing was also mentioned in the 1598 tithe dispute over Fornah Gill Close.

The Giggleswick historian T. Brayshaw wrote of an even more colourful episode in its history, one that took place in 1536. There had been a close association between Neals Ing and Sawley Abbey and at the Dissolution a number of local men became involved in the insurrection that history knows as the Pilgrimage of Grace. A bill on the church door at Giggleswick called on the rebels to meet at a place above Neals Ing – a private and remote rendezvous. We can picture them gathering at the farm before their ill-fated journey.

It might seem from all this that the history of Neals Ing goes back only to the early 1500s, but the etymology of the place-name suggests that it has a much longer history. The prefix derives from Neal, an old personal name that was formerly latinised as Nigellus and later gave rise to Nigel. This has always been a very unusual first name in Yorkshire, so much so that we can identify just a few families who used it in the Middle Ages, notably the de Plumptons and the de Stainforths. A connection with Nigel de Stainforth is therefore possible, directly or indirectly, for he was a prominent man in Ribblesdale in the late 1200s. His name appears frequently in the records of Sawley Abbey between *c.*1280 and 1304, so Neals Ing may originally have been his 'ing' or meadow.

There is a possible alternative. A family in Settle also used the name Nigel in the 1300s, probably kinsmen of the de Stainforths or allied to them through the god-parent relationship. A certain Nell de Hege was taxed in Settle in 1379, along with several individuals named Nellson or Neleson who were almost certainly his descendants. 'Hege' seems likely to be a variant spelling of 'Edge', which was itself an alternative name for Outmoor, the name of an enclosure that features in the title deeds for Neals Ing. The inference from 'de Hege' is that there was a settlement at Outmoor but I have been unable to discover anything about it.

The status of Neals Ing was far greater in the past than we might now imagine, as a case brought to the attention of the Skipton magistrates in 1703 makes clear. We need not here concern ourselves with

Skipton Castle in 1993. Prisoners were kept here from the time of King John, some later removed to York for trial, others held in custody by the Cliffords. The castle was slighted after its role in the Civil War but Lady Anne Clifford was responsible for its restoration about 1657. (*The author*)

the details of the debate but it is worth noting that Stainforth was described as a divided township consisting of four small villages, i.e. Great Stainforth and Neals Ing as one unit; Knight Stainforth and Feizor as another. It is surprising to find Neals Ing described as a village and even more surprising to find Feizor described as part of Stainforth township: usually it is linked with Clapham in the neighbouring wapentake of Ewcross. Each of the two was required to raise half the full rate for the township, although the residents of Knight Stainforth claimed that the lands in Great Stainforth were much underrated in value compared with theirs.

IMAGES AT AYSGARTH

Religious and political events of the Tudor period are still capable of polarising opinion and even historians have found themselves caught up in the great debates. It was Bindoff who said that the persecution of Protestants in Queen Mary's reign created martyrs on a scale previously unknown in England and was a 'drama which for good or ill was to remain one of the most vivid in the collective memory of the English people'. Rowse abandoned objectivity, railing against the iconoclasm of the Elizabethan bishops and the Protestants' destruction of things of beauty. He found repellent their desecration of chalices, images, the roods in their lofts, and stone altars, the so-called monuments of superstition. The Puritans were 'horrid', the Protestant mob 'disgusting', whilst the bishops had 'puffy, lined faces with ... constipated expressions, always grave, often sour'. In contrast, one Yorkshire gentleman was able to summarise the great changes that had taken place in his lifetime in an almost laconic manner: 'King Henry VIII and King Edward dyd putt downe the Masse, and sett upp the Comunyon. Qwene Mary dyd maynten the Masse again and now our sovereign Elezabeth hath sett upp the Holie Comunyon agayne', words written by John Kaye of Woodsome in his commonplace book.

It is in cases brought to the Ecclesiastical Courts that we obtain some insight into the impact that these events had on ordinary people. One detailed examination concerned the parishioners of Aysgarth: in 1567 Adam Wraye of Thoresby testified that when he had been ordered to see all the church books burnt he made a thorough search and obeyed his instructions although he could not say what the titles were. He also mentioned the order to deface and break 'all such images as remained in the churche', in particular the images of Mary and John. It becomes clear from several of the testimonies that an effort had been made to save these, for Adam Wraye was there when they were found hidden 'in the Roode loft of the churche'.

The minister Robert Hebblethwayte said that they had been concealed there 'in a valte or a hollow place' and he quite clearly disapproved of that. Adam Kirebye of Aysgarth recalled that initially the images had not been defaced but placed for safety 'in a lime kylne within the churcheyard'. Later, he saw his son Roger cut off one of the arms of the image of John whilst the image of Mary remained in a small enclosure belonging to John Deane where it was being used as a chopping block. Such was the zeal of Mr Hebblethwayte that he was also able to locate 'certeyn other latten books' that should have been destroyed and, in a chest within the choir, a number of forbidden items: 'one pix with the canapie which was wont to be hung over the same A crismatory and a little box for oyle A corporax with a case for the same'. Of course nobody admitted to knowing who had hidden these objects or planned their safe-keeping.

The Commissioners listened diligently to the depositions and it was decided that nine men had actively taken part in the attempt to preserve the proscribed items. As a result these nine were ordered to collect the images from the dwelling house of Sir Christopher Metcalfe, where they had been stored, and take them to 'the Church stele of Ayskarth' before the following Sunday. The ceremony that was planned for that day demonstrates the intention to humiliate the men publicly: they were to kneel in the choir of the church, facing the congregation 'bare headed bare footed and bare legged, havinge every one of theme a sheyte abowte him above his other apparel': they were then to repeat after the priest a full and abject apology. When that had been done they were to go back to the church stile 'and ther burne all the images' before the assembled parishioners.

J.S. Purvis has published other extracts from ecclesiastical records that serve to remind us of the passionate beliefs that divided Yorkshire communities in the sixteenth century. For example, in his account of disputes that arose over the occupation of pews and stalls in Slaidburn church, he told how the adherents of Cuthbert Musgrave and William Battersby of Slaidburn had repeatedly brawled in the aisles and pews to the 'greate desquyetting of divine service'. The depositions in this case tell us much of incidental importance about the history and status of the families involved but they also emphasise that such events might have had their origins in much earlier disputes, what Purvis referred to as 'a long and tangled tale of previous grievances or quarrels'. We are not accustomed now to thinking of the parish church as the scene of violence and blasphemous language, but the words used by those involved are preserved in these old documents.

SWINSTY HALL

Swinsty Hall has attracted the attention of numerous writers over the years, from William Grainge in 1895 to Louis Ambler, Edmund Bogg and Nikolaus Pevsner. In 1984, Barry Harrison and Barbara Hutton included it in their survey of vernacular houses in north Yorkshire, saying that the hall represented an important stage in the history of house building in the county, as a gentleman's residence with a ground-floor hall – the successor therefore to the tower houses of the late Middle Ages.

Swinsty Hall. The building in the foreground is the house where Walter Wood was living in 1540. It survived the building of the new hall thirty years later and was called the Old Hall in the inventory of 1639. It was saved from dereliction in the 1990s. (*The author*)

I suspect that few people make the connection between the place-name Swinsty Hall and its etymology but the meaning may originally have been 'pig sty'. Several identical names are on record in Yorkshire, including 'Swynsty hed' in Bilton (1438) and 'Swynstibek' in Guisborough (1338). The earliest example is 'Swinsty Bergh' in Tockwith, found in an undated twelfth-century charter. This is actually much earlier than the first mention of the word swine-sty in the OED, quoted from a document of 1340 where comparisons were being made between 'a kynges palays And a swynsty'. It is true that 'sty' as a suffix could also mean a path, as it does in the place-name and surname Hardisty, but the context here favours the first interpretation. We can only speculate how the pig-sty found itself transformed into a fine hall.

Walter Wode was said to be of 'Swynstie Haull' in 1540 and this is the earliest mention I have found of the place-name. It almost certainly has a much longer history and with 'hall' as a suffix the inference may be that Swinsty had lost its transparent meaning at an early date. The Woods enjoyed gentry status and they remained in residence at Swinsty Hall until the end of the century. It is tempting therefore to assume that Swinsty may have been their home from long before 1540, especially when they are named in connection with Little Timble. In 1379, for example, Walter del Wode was a carpenter in Little Timble, a married man taxed at the higher rate of 6d; Robert Wod of Timble 'in Otley' made his will in 1489 and Richard Wode of Timble, gentleman, died in 1523. Wood is a common surname but these Woods are likely to have been related, not least because Walter was used as a first name in both 1379 and 1540: indeed, it occurred again in 1570 when administration was granted for Walter Wode 'of Swynstie'. Parts of the family's late medieval hall survive, called the Old Hall in a later inventory. The present New Hall is said to have been erected by Francis Wood in 1575 as part of a marriage contract.

A more colourful but legendary explanation is that the builder of the hall had accumulated great riches in London by robbing the dead during a bout of plague but the only theme these two very different tales have in common is money. In order to finance the building of his new house, Francis Wood is said to have raised large sums of money from a Lancashire gentleman called Henry Robinson, and he forfeited the property when he could not make the repayments. Be that as it may, it is a fact that several documents which bear his name in those years had to do with money, e.g.

> 1581 Whereas one Mr Frauncis Woodd of Swinstiehall standith bound by his bill obligatorie in the some of fortie markes to me, the said Robert Pickerd, to surrender one parcel of ground called Stone Close in Tymble ... unto the uses of my fower daughters, etc.

According to historians the foreclosure on the house took place in 1590, and Henry Robinson occupied the premises soon afterwards. Nevertheless, 'Francis Wood of Swynestyehall' was one of three Fewston men named in a bond of £400 in 1593.

The Robinson family apparently remained at Swinsty Hall into the late eighteenth century and we can pick up references to them in Otley parish registers, deeds, wills and the correspondence of the Spencer Stanhopes. The initials of Henry Robinson and the date 1627 survive on the parlour window; Mr John Robinson was taxed on eight hearths on his house in Little Timble in 1672 and a child of Mr Edward Robinson's was buried at Fewston in 1738. The fees incidentally were paid to Otley church. Important as these references are in helping to build up a picture of the family's connection with the house, there is one document which more than any other brings Swinsty Hall to life, taking us back over 370 years to the house in its heyday.

When Henry Robinson died in 1639 he was buried at Fewston on 29 November and in his will he bequeathed the hall to his eldest son John. The majority of his goods were divided equally between two other children, Henry and Elizabeth. The inventory that accompanied the will is written on a vellum roll of three membranes and the appraisers take us through the fields, across the fold with its geese, pullen and 'two stone troughes', into the hall itself, moving from room to room. More than 350 animals were listed, with 'oxen, steares, kine, stirks, gimers, tupps, swine, weathers and meares': some of these were at a farm near by, possibly Redshaw, but others were specifically said to be 'att Hoame'. Sixty loads of oats and small amounts of wheat and rye were in storage and the winter corn was already growing in the fields. There were large quantities of hay in barns on different parts of the estate, valued at more than £24.

The appraisers visited eighteen or more rooms, many of them chambers or parlours, whilst others had clear working functions. In the 'shopp' there was equipment for cloth-making, together with yarn valued at £18. There were shears, three spinning wheels and 'two paire of Loames with on warping woaghe'. The kitchen had spits, racks, a dripping pan, a warming pan and numerous utensils made of pewter, brass, iron and 'panmettle'. There were servants' chambers, two butteries, a cellar, a milk house, an oven house with 'one cheese press' but no evidence of brewing. The items of furniture that were enumerated included no fewer than twelve tables, mostly 'little' but there were long tables with forms in the Old Hall and the Old Parlour, an old table in the kitchen and '1 leafe table' in the kitchen chamber. Beds were also numerous with no fewer than nine pairs of bedstocks. In the 'Shopp Chamber' were 'one stand bed and a truckle bed' and there were three feather beds in 'the chamber over the parlour', with bolsters, pillows and mattresses. This was where much of the household linen was also stored and items worthy of note here are 'fower dossen linen nabkins, fowerteen Coverletts of the best sort' and 'one longe quishing vallence

Swinsty Hall, built in 1570. Its renovation was started in the 1990s by Chris and Eileen Taylor. Previously, it had been owned by Leeds Corporation who had acquired it along with land needed for the Washburn valley reservoirs. (*The author*)

for one bed'. Scattered around the hall were a dozen chests and arks, four dressers, cupboards, buffet stools and chairs. A 'seald cheare' in the shop chamber and a 'sewed cheare' in the chamber over the parlour merit special mention, as do '1 desk, 1 counter and 1 presse for clothes' in the Old Hall. Some of this furniture was apparently still in the hall as late as 1895.

Individual items inside the house included tanned leather, two salting tubs, salt flesh, a stone morter and 'one kneading skeale'. In the outbuildings were pieces of old armour, walling hammers, wimbles, stone wedges and tools of every description: axes, gavelocks, a gouge, malls, chisels and a range of saws, i.e. 'one whipp Sage, two cutting Sages and one hand sage'. One or two paragraphs are of particular interest. For example a great deal of wood and timber was valued, including 'ynch Boards and seeleing boards in severall roomes, stoopes, Rayles for sealeing, Punchones for the same and sagen Bordes and all loose Sagen Timber in fower severall barnes ... and all other lose bords in and about the howse'. The reference to 'loose' timber and boards seems to suggest that much of the wood referred to fixtures such as panelling. Additionally there was 'fallen timber, part thereof lying upon Swinsty moore and the rest in the field and the felis' [fells?].

Among the husbandry items were three ploughs, four harrows, coulters, rakes, yokes, three scythes, eight sickles, a sowing hopp and a variety of carts, wains and two old sleds. The wains were for transporting turf, stone and hay and the coups had 'raths' to increase their capacity. Horse gear consisted of 'barkhooms, haimes, traces, teams and swingletrees', whilst 'three Loade Saddles with their furniture' are evidence that horses were also employed to move heavy goods. The specialist tools were turf spades, flaght spades and diking spades: shovels were listed but they were 'made and unmade', whilst 'speakes for wheels' and six pairs of wheels remind us that in winter it was usual to dismantle certain pieces of equipment.

SKYREHOLME

Skyreholme has attracted little attention from writers but aspects of its early history are revealed in two volumes published recently in the Record Series of the Yorkshire Archaeological Society. Most significant is the evidence that relates to the place-name in a twelfth-century charter for Bolton Priory. In the last quarter of that century, Alice de Rumilly confirmed a grant to Geoffrey de Neville of lands in Appletreewick that included an enclosure of more than 10 acres 'apud Skirum'. This takes the history of the place-name back several centuries earlier than the references quoted in PNWR and the spelling makes it clear that the meaning of the name must be re-interpreted. It is not an isolated example, for it occurs more than a dozen times in the Compotus of 1286–1325, spelt either Skyrom or Skyrum. These forms persisted into the 1600s.

The traditional explanation is that Skyreholme derives from two Scandinavian words with the meaning 'bright water-meadow' and the modern spelling seems to support that etymology. However, the earlier examples that are now available prove that 'Skyreholme' is a piece of popular etymology and that 'Skyrom' is the word that has to be explained. The transition is apparent in the seventeenth-century reference quoted in PNWR, i.e. '1602 Skyrom alias Skyreholme'. The name has precedents in Yorkshire: in Skiers Hall in Nether Hoyland, the first element is thought to derive from a word for a shed, in the sense of a poor dwelling. In that case the suffix -om or -um is likely to be a dative plural, so Skyrum should be interpreted as 'at the sheds'.

On Ian Kershaw's map of the Bolton Priory estate, Skyreholme is described as a stock farm, one of several in Appletreewick, and the accounts offer us a glimpse of developments there in the first two decades of the fourteenth century. From 1300 until 1315 the priory flourished but then poor harvests and raids by the Scots saw a dramatic decline in its fortunes and the entries reveal how that reverse affected Skyreholme. In the profitable years a stone wall was built around the old enclosure and newly-cleared land was secured by ditches and hedges. From 1303 there were good returns from hay harvests there, supervised by Thomas de Dibb. In 1313 Henry le Sclater was charged with putting a roof on the 'house' at Skyreholme and his by-name is of interest for it implies that the building was then substantial enough to warrant a stone slate roof.

Perhaps the first signs of decline are apparent in the references to repairs on the buildings there, with new roof repairs carried out as early as 1317. That was just after the famines and before the Scottish raids. As Skyreholme is not mentioned again for seven or eight years, a period during which the prior and most of the canons lived away from Bolton, it is possible that the farm lay uncultivated or was leased out at a very favourable rent. The absence of the name from the records tells

Bolton Priory, an Augustinian foundation. The first site was at Embsay in 1120, but the monks moved to Bolton soon after 1151. (*Author's collection*)

its own story but we know that the settlement continued to be a single dwelling for many years: in the priory rental of 1473 Henry Symson paid 20s as the tenant of 'one messuage at Skyrom', held in severalty. The same property is included in the accounts drawn up at the Dissolution when John Heleyes [Ellis?] held the lease of 'Skerome' paying 23s 4d rent.

Chapter 3

Place-Names and Surnames

The study of place-names and the study of surnames have tradition-ally been treated as distinct fields of research and yet there are major areas in which the two should not be separated, especially when the concern is with the numerous family names that derive from minor place-names. The reference works that are available to local and family historians often fail to mention these names or, more frustratingly, they provide information that is inadequate or inaccurate. In the following essays it is hoped to show how closely the two studies are linked and how together they open up topics of importance to genealogists, and historians more generally.

BATTERSBY – A 'DEPOPULATED' TOWNSHIP

The place-name Battersby occurs twice in Yorkshire, once in Cleveland and once in Bowland in the former West Riding: in both cases the first element is a distinctive Scandinavian personal name and the two names are identical in meaning. It has become usual for writers to describe Battersby in Bowland as 'a lost village' and to say that it was on the site of Battersby Barn in Slaidburn, also referred to as Battersby Farm, but there are good reasons for rejecting that identification and it is worth having another look at the evidence.

Few direct references to the name have been located in published sources but the starting point is the entry for 'Badresbi' in Domesday Book (1086). It was listed there among lands held by Earl Tosti which comprised Grindleton and twelve other localities, six of which would later come together as part of an extensive parish. These were Battersby, Easington, Hammerton, Newton, Radholme and Slaidburn, and it was Slaidburn that became the site of the parish church. Battersby then possessed two carucates of taxable land as did several of the other places named: it was a small estate but not smaller than many of its neighbours. Two of the localities in the same list have not been identified; that is *Bogeuurde* and *Sotleie*.

In Smith's *Place-Names of the West Riding* a paragraph is devoted to Battersby, with Battersby Farm as the head word and seven additional sourced references. It is a misleading list in two ways, firstly because no fewer than five of the examples were actually references to people called 'de Battersby', and these tell us nothing about the exact location of the settlement and are at best indirect evidence for the place-name. They start with William de Bathresby who was a witness to an un-dated charter for Sawley Abbey: this document is judged to have been written in the late twelfth century and it relates to places in Gisburn and Rimington, not to Slaidburn. The other surname examples are from the period 1316 to 1379 and I propose to set these aside for the moment and concentrate on the two claimed place-name references. One can be dismissed immediately, that is 'Battersbye 1607', for when we examine the context it is clear that it refers to Battersby in Cleveland – a second misleading item.

The only one of Smith's examples that can be directly attributed to Battersby in Bowland is taken from the survey of 1285 that we know as *Kirkby's Inquest*. The full entry is 'Neuton in Bogheland cum Batersby', two vills treated as one unit which between them possessed three carucates of land; that is exactly half the total of the same two places at the time when Domesday Book was compiled. The inference seems to be that Battersby had lost its independent status by that date and may already have been partially depopulated, although it is difficult to say why. Similar examples of depopulation were described by Maurice Beresford as mysterious. What can be said is that the Black Death cannot be blamed and that Battersby was not the only place locally to suffer that fate. If we are right to place the loss of status between 1086 and 1285 it happened during a period when the population generally was on the increase.

Slaidburn was listed separately in both 1285 and 1316 and the entry in *Kirkby's Inquest* focuses our attention on the connection that Battersby had with Newton. Evidence in the *Nomina Villarum* of 1316 appears to confirm the link, for the survey contains no entry for Battersby as a place-name but has Newton in the possession of Richard de Bathersby. As we have seen above, the surname or by-name had first been recorded in the late twelfth century and its survival in Newton may point to the family's occupation of the territory throughout that period. Battersby was linked with Newton in 1367, in a Kirkstall Abbey document, and in 1572 when Nicholas Battersbye, gentleman, sold a substantial property to two men called Wynder and Bradshawe. In the fine which records the transaction the estate was described as the 'Manor of Battersbye and 20 messuages with lands in Battersbye, Newton and Essington'. Apart from those references there is no mention of the place-name in the wide range of documents that has been searched, including wills, fines, court rolls, inquisitions and the parish registers.

The editor of *Kirkby's Inquest* named 'Battrix' or modern Beatrix as the site of Battersby; no doubt influenced by the fact that it has the same Scandinavian personal name as its first element. It proved an attractive theory to some historians, notably to Beresford who accepted the identification and described Battersby as 'an extinct place two miles west of Newton in Bowland'. That cannot be correct, although there may have been a link between the two names from soon after the date of settlement: Beatrix could have been a site where Battersby men had a cattle-raising farm or grazed their animals in summer. More recently the late Mary Higham challenged the traditional interpretation of Beatrix in two articles that have now been republished.

The early history of the Battersby family confirms their link with the Domesday vill and points to a more likely location for the 'lost' village. Effectively, that history begins with the information in the poll tax returns of 1379: there are scattered references to the surname in Bowland before then but it is only in 1379 that we have clear evidence about where members of the family lived and their status. Three tax-payers had the surname and the wealthiest was Richard de Bathersby of Newton who paid 2s. Easington was the home of Roger de Bathersby: he paid 12d and had the title of 'franklin', a designation that identified him as a freeman and landowner, just below 'gentry' level. A single lady called Alice de Bathersby lived at Long Preston where she paid the standard rate of 4d. The Battersbys were clearly one of the more prominent families in the district, with lands in Newton and Easington, and tax lists from the Tudor period confirm that they still held that position in the first half of the sixteenth century. In 1547, for example, Nicholas Battersbie of Newton was taxed 20s on lands or income valued at £10. In view of the fine of 1572, mentioned earlier, it seems safe to assume that the family's property included 'the Manor of Battersby'.

The interior of Slaidburn church has many treasures, especially the impressive rood screen, the box pews and the three-decker pulpit. The pew for Dunnow preserves a link with the 'lost' vill of Battersby. (*The author*)

The research of Chris Spencer into the manorial records of Slaidburn has brought new information about the place-name to light. In the court rolls of the early seventeenth century, there is frequent mention of Battersby Hall as an alias for Dunnow, a locality between Slaidburn and Newton that lies close to the river. The estate was owned at that time by Richard Sherburne, the illegitimate son of Richard Sherburne of Stonyhurst who had bequeathed the property to him in his will of 1594. This points to the present house at Dunnow as the likely site of the Domesday vill.

Battersby survives therefore only as a surname, well established in both Yorkshire and Lancashire but far more numerous now in the latter county. It was still popular in Ribblesdale in 1672 and it was there that much of the expansion took place. By 1881 there were good numbers in Blackburn, Clitheroe and Preston but even bigger con-centrations in Leigh (297), Wigan (150) and Bolton (144). There were smaller but significant Yorkshire groups in Airedale, Leeds and Sheffield. Battersby in the North Riding gave rise to a by-name but there is no evidence that it survived and the surname was not recorded in that part of Yorkshire in 1672.

BEECROFT HALL

There are several localities in the Dales that are named Beecroft or which have Beecroft as part of the place-name. Professor Smith was right to say that Beecroft Moor in Timble probably owed its name to the Beecroft family for they were prominent in the parish from the mid-1500s. However, he took three similar names at face value, interpreting them as crofts 'where bees were kept', that is Beecroft in Wigglesworth, Beecroft Hall in Horton in Ribblesdale and Bee Croft in Thornton in Lonsdale. That seems unlikely in the case of Beecroft in Wigglesworth which was known originally as 'Beecrofts' and is almost certainly named after the family: William Becrofte who was a tenant of Mr Hamerton lived there as early as 1522. The two other places named Beecroft were both settlements in the sixteenth century and either could be the source of the surname. The Horton name seems the more likely but the two place-names have identical spellings and their etymology is the key to the surname's meaning.

The modern spelling Beecroft developed from 'Bigcroft' and a family with that name lived in Horton in the fourteenth century: in 1379 William de Bygcrofft and his wife were taxed 4d there whilst Robert Bygcroft, also a married man, paid 4d tax at Gisburn further down the valley. I have not been able to discover when the family left Horton but two examples from Appletreewick rentals demonstrate the change in the spelling, i.e. 1473 Robert Bigcroft; 1539 Robert Becroft. Some members of the family took the surname much further afield and by the mid-1600s there were Beecrofts throughout the western dales and in a few other parts of Yorkshire. The meaning is therefore straightforward: Scandinavian *bygg* was the usual word in the Dales for barley so Beecroft can be explained as 'barley croft'. Bee Croft in Thornton had the same early spelling but its history has been traced back only to *c.*1600 when a branch of the Tatham family lived there.

These surnames are actually the earliest evidence we have at this stage for the place-name. Until the Dissolution, 'the manor of Bigcroft', together with the tithes of the church in Horton in Ribblesdale, belonged to the nunnery of Clementhorpe in York: it may have been included in property granted to them by the de Staveleys as early as the mid-1200s. However, the place-name's linguistic history runs parallel to that of the surname, as we discover once members of the Howson family have been identified as tenants of the hall or manor house. They were said to be of 'Bigcrofte' in Horton in 1534 and of 'Becrofte Hall' in 1593. In a deed of 1615 the name of the property was given as Bycroft alias Beacroft and these alternative spellings have clear implications for the development of the surname.

Indeed, with the exception of the early spelling Bigcroft, those forms of the place-name are reflected in variants of the surname. A man who can be traced as a resident of Leeds between 1545 and 1582 was recorded there in wills and in the parish registers as Edward Becroft, Beacroft, Beecroft and Bicroft; in 1543 Thomas Becrofte and Christopher Bicrofte were both taxed in Halton West. A more unusual variant may be Pycroft, found in Linton parish register in 1608, but no alias has yet been identified and this name may have an alternative origin, possibly in Norfolk. Beecraft, Becraft and Bycraft are all uncommon.

The reference works either fail to mention these names or offer misleading explanations: Bycroft has always been taken literally; that is 'by the croft': Reaney interpreted it in that way in 1967 and Weekley referred to it in 1917 as 'the obvious Bycroft'. The recently updated *Penguin Dictionary of Surnames* (2009) makes no mention of Beecroft, Bycroft or Pycroft. This lack of information cannot be because the surname is uncommon, for it is well documented and its total nationally in 1881 was close to 2,000.

COWGILL HOUSE – A LOST PLACE-NAME

The narrow lane that leads east and then north east out of Malham, heads initially for Gordale, then climbs via Hawthorne Lane and Smearbottoms Lane to the farm called Lee Gate. This is a place-name with a long and complicated history and it takes us back to a very early phase of settlement on the moor. The complications arise partly because of a change in the name and partly because the farm lies close to the boundary that once divided Malham from Burnsall. Indeed, in old documents Lee Gate is sometimes described as being in Hetton or in Rylstone, both of which were formerly in Burnsall parish. Unfortunately, there is no easy or entertaining way of presenting the evidence that establishes the name's origin but the correct identification is of considerable importance to local and family historians so perhaps I may be forgiven for pursuing each twist and turn in the story.

We begin with the place-name Lee Gate in its present form, and this takes us back some 350 years at least. Among the earliest examples are entries in Rylstone parish registers in the 1700s and a document in the Raistrick collection, dated 1653. Alternative spellings in that period were 'Lee Yate' and 'Leeyeat', sometimes written as one word, sometimes as two. These arise from the colloquial pronunciation of 'gate' and they confirm that we are dealing with the word in the sense of a moveable barrier, not in the sense of a road or highway. The first derives from an Old English word and the second from a Scandinavian word, and there are numerous instances of both elements in local place-names.

It is in the spellings of the late 1500s and early 1600s that we have evidence of an important development in the name's history. This is illustrated in two examples from the registers of Kirkby Malham, that is 'Hothorne Lid Yeat' (1603) and 'Hawthorne Leigheyeate' (1597). It seems clear that we owe the prefix 'Hawthorne' to the nearby Hawthorne Lane, and we can consider the implications of that later, but the spelling 'Lid Yeat' is of great significance, since the word 'lidyate' was widely used in the past for a swing gate. Such gates were designed to prevent animals from straying, and were typically located near a settlement, in fences that divided rough grazing from arable or from cultivated land. The term fits in well with the location of the farm, positioned close to a lane that leads from Malham over to Mastiles Lane.

The Malham court roll of 1534 contains the earliest reference to the place-name in this form that I have noted. On 11 August that year the townsmen were accused of failing to make 'the defences between Hawthornelydyate and Netherhawthorne Lydyate', despite having been ordered to do so previously. If the first of these lay close to the farm, then the 'nether' or lower gate may have been further down the lane, closer to Malham. In any case it raises the possibility that 'Lydgate' was the original form of Lee Gate and Professor Smith settled for that explanation in *Place-Names of the West Riding of Yorkshire*. Unfortunately, we cannot dismiss the recurring element 'lee' so easily.

These alternative versions of the place-name, that is Lydgate and Lee Gate, can be traced back at least to the Dissolution for, when the Fountains Abbey lands were sold to Sir Richard Gresham in 1540, the farm we are concerned with was referred to as 'Hawthorne Lydyate', whereas a few years earlier, in a survey of the estate, it was called 'Hawthorn Leyse' which seems likely to be a form of 'lee' or 'ley' and is possibly a significant spelling. The property at that time consisted of two tenements which were in the occupation of John and Henry Thompson – useful evidence since the surname of the tenants helps us to be sure that we are talking about one farm and not two. For example, when Henry Thompson made his will, in 1552, he was said to be 'of Haythorne Lyeate'. From a variety of sources it is possible to trace the Thompson family as tenants of the farm back to *c*.1450, but the link may go back even further, since a man called Adam Tomson was taxed in Malham in 1379.

Unless earlier evidence comes to light, we are left to speculate which of the alternatives is the 'real' name, that is whether 'Lidyate' became 'Leeyate' and then Lee Gate or whether 'Leesyate' became temporarily 'Lydyate'. But that is not the end of the story. In 1535 John and

Lee Gate, Malham, farmed now by the Carr family. It is on the site of Cowgill House, a property that was part of the Fountains Abbey estate. (*The author*)

Henry Thompson were said to be tenants of 'Cogilhouse otherwise Hawthorne Leyse': in 1540 this was rendered as 'Cogylhouse alias dict. Hawthorne Lydyate'. Whilst these aliases help to confirm that 'Leyse' and 'Lydyate' were just alternatives of the same place-name, they also introduce us to 'Cogilhouse', a further variation.

There is proof in the records of Fountains Abbey that this was the farm's original name. In 1495–96, for example, the rental had Robert Thompson as the tenant of a moiety, or half, of the lodge of 'Cogilhouse' and Thomas Thompson as the tenant of the other moiety. The sum of their rents was 26s 8d, exactly the valuation placed on the farm in the 1535 survey. In the bursar's accounts of the abbey there are several references to the farm in 1446–58, including a mention of the widow of William Thompson 'de Colgilhous'. I have no earlier examples of the place-name but the 'l' that we find in this last spelling links it with the 'de Colgill' family: in 1379, several members of this family were taxed in Malham and townships close to Malham Moor. By the 1500s, the 'l' of Colgill was neither written nor pronounced although it may have survived longer in the family name. For example, a certain John Colgill of Ilkley made his will as late as 1521. Not long afterwards the spelling stabilised as Cowgill.

Finally, therefore, we can say that today's Lee Gate is on the site of a medieval settlement and that the present name is merely the latest in its long history. Also part of the story is Lee Gate's derelict neighbour, Cow Gill Cote, with spellings parallel to those of Cowgill House in the Middle Ages. The two are only half a mile apart, on opposite sides of Cow Gill Beck, a stream that has its source on the moorland immediately to the north. This is clearly seen on the current OS map, and the inference is that both settlements took their name from the 'gill' that separates them. It seems possible therefore that 'Cowgill', as a territory, is much older than the documentary evidence suggests and might go back to a time before the boundary that placed them in different parishes was established. In any event it seems likely that the gill was named before the settlements.

On current maps the name Cow Gill Beck applies only to the short and relatively flat stretch of the stream that descends from the moor to the two farms mentioned, or just beyond. Downstream from that point it is now called Bordley Beck, flowing southwards to join up with the river Aire. However, if we take into account the meaning of 'gill', used

In 2007, a group of American Cowgills visited Malham. They were descendants of a family that left England for Pennsylvania in 1682. Here, Perry Cowgill, on the right, and Frank Carr who farms at Lee Gate, look across to Cow Gill Cote. (*The author*)

for a ravine or deep cleft, we might conclude that Bordley Beck has more recently replaced 'Colgill' as the name for the deeply-cut stretch of the valley south of the farms. If that were true it could affect the etymology, for the prefix *col* is far from straightforward. It has three possible interpretations and the early spellings are not distinctive enough for us to prefer one over the others on linguistic grounds. It could be the Middle English equivalent of our modern words 'cool' or 'coal', or even the Scandinavian personal name *Kolli*, found as the first element in place-names such as Coleby. The last of these would imply that the gill was named in the pre-Conquest phase of Scandinavian settlement or very soon afterwards. Initially, I thought it most unlikely that the first element could be 'coal', as limestone is so dominant in the landscape, but in fact there was coal lower down the gill and two early minor names, that is 'Bordley coal pits' (1656) and 'the Colepitt gill' (1671), now make this a credible interpretation.

I can only speculate about the disappearance of the original name Colgill House and the later confusing aliases. One possibility is that they came into use because Hawthorne Lee or Lees was the name of a clearance near to or adjoining the farm: a title deed of 1573 actually refers to Richard and Robert Thompson of Haythorneleye, as though that were the name of the farm. I believe 'lidyate' was a mistake, an early example of popular etymology, given credibility because it is such a common Yorkshire place-name and fits the location. There would almost certainly have been a gate on the lane at that point and Hawthorne Lees Yate might easily have been misinterpreted as Hawthorne Lidyate – the second alias. It is, though, the element 'lee' that survives in the modern name Lee Gate.

As a surname Cowgill has received little attention, although it is still quite numerous in both Yorkshire and Lancashire. There is no entry for it in Reaney & Wilson and the Penguin Dictionary simply says that there are five places named Cowgill in the West Riding, suggesting four possible interpretations.

FAWBER

The tiny hamlet of Fawber is in Ribblesdale, and it lies beyond New Houses, just to the east of the old highway from Horton to High Birkwith. The buildings are partly protected from the weather by a ridge to the east and there is a spring close by, but this is now an isolated spot. Direct references to the place-name take its history back into the 1500s but I have no doubt that the settlement goes back even further, to the early fourteenth century at least. There is evidence for that in the name Robert de Falbergh of Horton who is mentioned in a Furness Abbey charter of *c*.1338: the inference is that he took his name from where he was living. The two elements of the place-name can be identified as *(ge)fall*, a place where trees had been felled and *berg*, a hill. Perhaps the clearance, like so many others, had been made in the thirteenth century as the population was increasing.

If that was the case there is no evidence that the family remained for any length of time at Fawber, although they can be traced to communities quite near by later in the century. The farm may even have been temporarily abandoned after the Black Death, and when we finally locate the Fawber family it is as tenants of Bolton Priory. In an account roll of 1377–78 John Falbergh was one of three men mentioned

The ford and clapper bridge at New Houses, formerly on the route from Horton in Ribblesdale to Fawber, High Birkwith and Ling Gill, that joined the highway over Cam Fell. The stream was dry in June 2005 when this picture was taken. (*The author*)

in connection with the sub-cellarer and, in 1422, a man of the same name served as a juror at Skipton. He acted as a witness in an inquisition into the lands of John de Clifford, killed at the siege of Meaux. There is a will for John Falbargh of Bolton in Craven in the registry at York, dated 1430, but I cannot say how long the family remained in the parish. The priory rental for 1473 contains one further reference to the surname but it is missing from the Dissolution rental.

Later, the surname occurs in various parts of the Dales and in several prominent Yorkshire towns, all some distance from Fawber itself. The spellings vary considerably, which may imply that the clerks who were responsible no longer associated the surname with the place-name. The way it developed can be seen in a sequence of references to a family in Newton in Bowland. In the subsidy roll of 1543, Robert Falber was taxed 2d there and a widow Falber, who may have been his mother, paid 4d. Her deceased husband had been called Ralph, a favourite name in this branch of the family. A second Ralph Falber witnessed the will of William Marton of Newton in 1594 and a third was taxed there on a house with four hearths in 1672. His surname on that occasion was spelt Faber.

This surname is usually said to derive from the Latin word *faber* which means a blacksmith, and there are certainly men referred to as 'le faber' in early documents. I suppose this has to be considered as a possible source of the name, although the examples quoted are almost always from early Latin documents and there is no satisfactory evidence which demonstrates how and why a Latin word became an English surname. In fact there seems to be no evidence that 'faber' was ever a word in general use and it does not appear in the OED. Alternatively, as Faber was a surname known on the Continent it may sometimes have had an overseas origin.

There can be no doubt, though, that in Yorkshire Faber was a variant of Falber and Fawber wherever the family settled. In Leeds, for example, Abraham Fawbar married Elizabeth Iles in 1579 and he was a witness, as Abraham Faber, to the will of her father Edward in 1586. When his wife was buried, in 1588, he was referred to as Abraham Fawbert, the name having a final 't' on that occasion. This would eventually become the usual form of the surname. A direct connection between the Leeds man and a family in York seems likely. A tallow chandler called Abraham Fawber was enrolled as a freeman of York in 1596 and he subsequently held the office of chamberlain: in 1619 he was entered in the rolls as Abraham Faber, chandler. In 1645, another Abraham Faber featured in the rolls: he was also a tallow chandler. In the hearth tax of 1672 the family had gentry status and a Mr Faber was taxed on six hearths in the parish of St John the Evangelist.

Fawber was not a prolific surname, even if we take all the variants into account, but it did expand modestly in the parish of Kirkby Malzeard. George Fawber or Faber is the first on record, in 1580, and generations of his family were tenants there to the Elsleys. In 1614 a certain Thomas Faber was responsible for a bastard child born to Jane Woodward of Clint, and she was ordered to be taken to Ripley on market day, 'stripped naked from the midle upwards and ... soundly whipped through the towne'. Thomas escaped this punishment but was made responsible for the child's education.

The Kirkby Malzeard family may have been closely related to Brian Fawber of Grantley who died in 1590, for some of the title deeds to their property refer to other families called Fawber in Ripon and Sleningford. Exactly the same variations in spelling are found in this

The tiny hamlet of Fawber, once on an ancient highway but isolated since the building of the new road through Selside to Ribblehead. (*The author*)

parish as elsewhere, and John Fawber or Fawbert is mentioned in 1698–1703. In the hearth tax of 1672 George Faubert and Thomas Fawber were living in the township and there were other individuals with the surname in Bishop Monkton and Ripon.

The lack of expansion is apparent in the census statistics for 1881 when there were a mere 217 Fawberts in Britain. Of these 106 were in the West Riding, with one significant cluster in Bradford (61) and smaller numbers in Ripon and Leeds, areas traditionally associated with the name. Elsewhere in Yorkshire there were another 87 Fawberts, with York (28) and Helmsley (14) as the most important locations. Darlington accounted for almost all those who lived out-side the county and in that respect it is worth noting that a William Fawbarte died in Stokesley in 1546. In 1881, there were also 18 Fauberts, shared between Bradford and Leeds, and a single Fauber, in London. However, Faubert like Faber can have a Continental origin. Almost as common as Fawbert was Faber (200), most of these living in London and only a modest number in Yorkshire (15). At this stage we can only speculate how many of these were variants of Fawber.

NUSSEY HOUSE, APPLETREEWICK

Nussey House lies on Appletreewick Moor, on the great highway that crosses Greenhow Hill en route to Pateley Bridge and Ripon. It is an ancient place-name, recorded from the end of the twelfth century: in 1172–90, Alice de Rumilly confirmed a grant of land in Appletreewick to Geoffrey Neville and part of this concerned an enclosure of 5½ acres 'apud Nuscey'. It is next mentioned in 1298 when an agreement between the abbot of Fountains and James de Eston confirmed the abbey's right to 'free transit and chase' through the lands of Appletreewick. Included in the grant was common pasture to the north of a highway which went from 'Cravenkeld usque Nussay heved', that is Nussey Head. The antiquity of the route, older by far than the place-name, is confirmed by the discovery 'among the stones of the moor' of a Roman pig of lead. On it was an inscription which included the name TRAJAN.

The economic success of Bolton Priory towards the end of the thirteenth century resulted in the acquisition of lands which included the manor of Appletreewick. This purchase, in 1300, gave the priory access to extensive areas of pasture on the moors, and it immediately began to expand its stock-rearing activities there. The setting up of a sheep farm or 'bercary' at Nussey was just one of several enterprises in that district: a piggery was built there soon afterwards and just to the north, at Grimwith and Gateup, new vaccaries or cattle farms were also established. Ian Kershaw described such bercaries as 'moorland lodges for the shepherds, sheep-cotes and pens, with facilities for dipping, shearing, and milking, and with nearby meadow closes and large surrounds of pasture'.

What we know about Nussey's early history has to be gleaned from the financial records of the priory, and these accounts provide us with revealing insights into daily life there in the earliest decades of the fourteenth century: there are references to hay-making, to the erection of an enclosure fence, the digging of ditches and the building of stone walls. Isolated items relate to the manure that was cleaned out of the folds to be used as fertilizer, to the carriage of ferns and heather, possibly for animals' bedding, and to eight sheep killed in a great storm in 1321. The herdsmen at Nussey are mentioned almost incidentally, as when they received gratuities of grain, or food and drink, but more frequent are details of expenses incurred in building, or building repairs. In 1318–19, for instance, expensive repairs to Nussey House (*domus de Nuscey*) are a reminder of damages suffered in the raids south by Scotsmen, in the wake of their victory at Bannockburn.

By contrast, information about events up to the Dissolution is confined to one or two isolated references. In the priory rental of 1473 it was 'occupied by sheep' and the bercary there consisted of 12 acres of enclosed meadow and a house with common pasture: the valuation was 44s. In the Dissolution rental of 1538–39 the income was 26s 8d which accrued from 'the farm of 1 house called Nussehouse ... in the tenure of William Crofte by indenture'. Throughout this early period it is clear that the settlement was known as Nussey House so it is interesting to find it described as 'The Grange of Nussey Howse' in 1623 when it was sold by John Yorke of Gouthwaite to Mr William Steile. Nussey had not been a grange of the priory so this manipulation of the name may have been an early attempt at 'gentrification'.

The colloquial pronunciation of the place-name was subtly different, as we discover in a case of sheep-stealing dealt with by the magistrates at Skipton in 1700. It concerned Thomas Gill 'of Nursa House' who claimed that one of his wethers had gone missing: he suspected William Greene of Greenhow Hill and, knowing the man's habits, went to see if he could find the sheep. In his own words he discovered it 'hung up in a grove hole under ground', that is in an old lead mine. Greene did not deny the offence but claimed that 'hunger compelled him'. More officially, a map of Yorkshire dated 1771 has 'Nursa Knot' as the name of the hill behind the settlement, probably the limestone knoll where the pig of lead was discovered.

The interpretation of the place-name takes into account the earliest spellings and the references to Nussey Head. We know that Nussey was already a territory by the twelfth century, with a top enclosure and a bottom enclosure. These had a combined total of 11½ acres and the boundaries would have included today's Knot Head, together with Nussey House and Nussey Green. The variations in spelling are ambiguous, for 'Nuscehay' and 'Nushaye' seem to refer to an enclosure, possibly Old English (*ge*)*haeg* whilst 'Notesaiheved' in the charter of 1172–90 could be interpreted as 'nut shaw' or copse. The word knot in the sense of hill is found principally in the north-west of England and is probably Scandinavian in origin. It is difficult to be certain for it occurs mostly in place-names for which no early material has been noted.

Nussey House Farm on the road over Greenhow Hill that leads to Pateley Bridge.
Just visible on the left is part of Nussey Knot – called Nursery Knot on recent
Ordnance Survey maps. (*The author*)

The rare surname Nussey clearly derives from the settlement for it is
recorded in Appletreewick from the 1370s, although there is nothing to
link the family directly to the 'bercary'. A few examples will confirm
the presence of the surname in the township: John de Nussay was
taxed there in 1379 and Thomas Nussay, a tenant of Bolton Priory, held
a messuage and 3 bovates of land there in 1473. Robert Nussey paid 2s
tax in Appletreewick in 1543 and the name then features in Burnsall
parish registers into the seventeenth century. Another Robert Nussey
was listed in the Appletreewick hearth tax of 1672.

Happily, a Quarter Sessions' deposition allows us to eavesdrop on
an everyday conversation that Robert had in 1675 when he was
returning 'upon Mayday ... from the faire holden at Rippon'. He told
the magistrates how he had fallen into the company of James Shaw of
'Greenhaw Hill', and had spent some time with him, discussing 'the
dearness of goodes at the Faire'. In the document he signed himself

'Nusse' but was named as Robert Nursey and this spelling points the way to a significant variant. It has a long history and probably reflects the colloquial pronunciation of the place-name.

The registry of wills at York has an entry for John Nussay alias Nursay in 1508 and in Wragby parish register George Nussey can be identified as George Nursey in the period 1799–1806. It was not the only variation, for Nurse, Nurser and Nursaw can also be found in the records: Agnes Nurse, who died in 1509, was the widow of John Nussay and Robert Nursay or Nurssa of Birthwaite in Ripley featured in another case at the Quarter Sessions in 1680. That is not to say that Nurse and Nurser can always be linked with Nussey but they were certainly occasional variants, via Nursey.

They also help to explain a number of minor place-names. One branch of the Nusseys had moved into Bradford by the early 1500s, for William Nussie of Manningham made a bequest of 3s 4d to Burnsall church in 1521: John Nussey was named in a muster roll there in 1539. Nurser Lane is an unexplained Bradford name listed by Smith. In his section on the field names for Ripley there is Nursaw Close which he suggested might be a late spelling of 'Nordscow' (north wood), recorded in the twelfth century. It seems far more likely to have been named after the family of the Robert Nurssa of Ripley referred to earlier.

In 1881, Nussey was still far more common in Yorkshire than anywhere else. The national total of 196 was very modest but 84 per cent of these lived in the West Riding, notably in an area defined roughly as Leeds, Dewsbury and Wakefield. Early examples of the surname in the registers for that part of the Riding include: 1580 Humphrey Nussye of Leeds Townend and 1589 John Nuccye of Thornhill. Edward Nusse of Birstall (1609) was said by the editor of the register, John Nussey, to be from Bradford. However, all three major variants, that is, Nursay, Nursaw and Nursey were by then less common in Yorkshire than in other counties. Nursey, easily the most numerous (215), occurred more frequently in East Anglia than in Yorkshire where Leeds was again its main 'home'; Nursay (8) occurred principally in Tynemouth (Northumberland) whereas Nursaw (31) was more common in Buckinghamshire. There was one small cluster in York (8) where Mr Thomas Nursaw, a grocer, had been registered as a freeman in 1747. There may be alternative origins for these surnames, but the probability is that they represent the early dispersal of the Yorkshire surname.

Chapter 4

Surname Histories

Traditionally, surname studies have been treated as the domain of the etymologist and there can be no doubt that the meaning of a name is what concerns most people. It should be said though that many of the historic interpretations of surnames have now been shown to be flawed, largely because of the methods employed by etymologists, and the result is that the standard dictionaries are unreliable. The context in which a surname originated is vital to our understanding of its meaning but for that to be relevant to the family historian a clear link must be established with the modern surname. That basic principle has often been ignored by those who compile dictionaries of surnames.

Ideally there should be genealogical evidence to help identify the progenitors but in many cases that will simply not be possible and some origins will remain unsolved. In its absence a sequence of examples, linked by relationship and supporting data, is often the only practical alternative. We cannot always avoid speculating about a name's meaning but the point where evidence has given way to guesswork should be made clear. This approach to surname study means that family historians now need to take into account any information that throws light on a surname, including topics such as expansion, decline, distribution, migration and linguistic development. The increasing use of DNA presents genealogists with new opportunities and new challenges.

It would clearly be difficult for a national dictionary to treat surnames in such depth but the methods I have just outlined should remain the ideal, and genealogical research should underpin the etymologies suggested. This approach has already been used in the investigation into the links between place-names and the surnames derived from them: I propose now to examine a wider variety of surnames in order to emphasise that point.

EXPANSION AND ORIGIN

It is not generally realised how many of our best-known surnames are extremely uncommon. Stephen Archer has now provided us with that information, employing statistics drawn from the census of 1881. His ground-breaking CD, *The British 19th Century Surname Atlas,* tells us which names have ramified in this country in the course of their history and which have barely survived. There are many surprises. Some names that are household words are revealed as being quite rare, e.g. Wogan (84), Dibnah (99) and Trescothick (4). If we think only of broadcasters' names the national totals for Cleese (12), Peston (7) and Inverdale (4) provide evidence of names on the brink of extinction. They can be contrasted dramatically with names which are prolific and yet appear to have a single family origin, such as Schofield (16,259), Greenwood (23,256) and Sykes (14,383). In the case of Sykes the use of DNA evidence has already confirmed the possibility of a single source in west Yorkshire.

It was Camden, with his description of Metcalfe as the 'familia numerosissima totius Angliae', who first drew attention to the successful expansion of this surname. That expansion initially took place in Wensleydale and the exciting prospect for those with Metcalfes in their ancestry is the possibility that they share a single family origin. They certainly appear to owe the name to one person. The earliest examples on record are: 1301 Adam Medecalf' of Bainbridge and 1379 John Metcalf of Mallerstang. It is not possible at this stage to say whether Adam Medecalf' was the first to bear the name but no evidence has yet been brought forward to suggest that it has an alternative source. Even so, the meaning is not at all obvious and various suggestions have been put forward over the years. Not surprisingly, some of the theories do not stand up to scrutiny.

Others are more worthy of consideration. Sir Anthony Wagner was one of several writers who speculated that the source might be 'the mountain called Calf' near Sedbergh, but the location of the hill, the lack of early evidence for the place-name, and the fact that the first examples of the surname are not consistent with a place-name origin, make this unconvincing. Reaney discussed some of the other possibilities, including the theory that it might have referred to a calf turned out into the meadow to be fattened for eating. A surname which lends some support to that suggestion has been located in the Coucher Book of Selby, i.e. 1270 Simon Croftcalf of Rawcliffe. On the face of it this

Nappa Hall. This postcard view from the early 1900s shows the defensible west tower and the lower kitchen block to the east. The hall is said to have been built by the Metcalfes in 1459 and it remained in the family's possession for over 300 years. (*Author's collection*)

could have a similar meaning and it is clear from the records that it became hereditary in that district. Unlike Metcalfe, though, it did not survive for very long and was noted only by local historians.

The eventual ramification of the Metcalfe 'clan' has been the stuff of legends from an early date: when Sir Anthony Wagner speculated in *English Genealogy* (1960) that all the Metcalfes might be 'of one stock', he recalled Leland's comment on Sir James Metcalfe who died in 1589; there were, he said, 300 men of his 'knowen consanguinitie'. That may have been an exaggeration but a variety of records prove how prolific the family was in Wensleydale, certainly from the seventeenth century. In and around Bainbridge the expansion was certainly remarkable; in the hearth tax returns of 1673, for example, no fewer than seventy taxpayers listed under Bainbridge bore the surname, with many more in neighbouring parishes. The total in the North Riding alone was over 170.

Metcalfe has long been the preferred spelling. In 1881 the national total was 6,867, and only 617 British surnames were more popular. It is a remarkable expansion, for the majority of the more common names, unlike Metcalfe, certainly had plural or multiple family origins. The statistics confirm how great the ramification had been in the northern dales, with 523 Metcalfes listed in Aysgarth and 245 in Skipton: the much smaller communities of Reeth (Swaledale) and Settle (Ribblesdale) had 169 and 177 respectively. The surname was prolific too in the industrial areas of the West Riding, with 426 in Bradford and 264 in Leeds, and it had spread far beyond Yorkshire, for over 3,000 examples were recorded elsewhere: it was predictably popular in Lancashire (812) and Durham (717) but rare in both Scotland and Wales.

These numbers do not tell the whole truth about the name's expansion, for the obvious variants included one or two that were also numerous. In order of frequency they were: Metcalf 6,065; Medcalf 1,171; Medcalfe 123; Midcalf 102; Mitcalf 40; Mitcalfe 14 and Midcalfe 6. The least common spellings usually occurred outside Yorkshire but together they raise the total number of 'Metcalfes' in 1881 to 14,388. If the spelling had not varied, few distinctive British surnames would have had higher totals. Surprisingly, no examples of the dialect spellings of the surname appear to have survived, although they feature regularly in the parish registers, e.g. 1605 Edward Mecka of Leeds; 1740 Sarah Meccah of Hartshead.

Alderson is a surname that has received little attention and yet it has a long and fascinating history in the northern Pennines where it is still extremely common. The pattern of its distribution in 1881 is a reflection of that history, with Durham and Yorkshire accounting for almost seventy-five per cent of the national total of 4,154. The statistics from the census, nationally and regionally, tell part of the story: Yorkshire 1,648; Durham 1,252; Lancashire 355; Westmorland 146.

Of course, what these totals fail to show is how popular the surname was in parts of those areas, but Stephen Archer provided statistics for the districts of the Poor Law unions which identify the major concentrations. They show that it was in the North Riding that Aldersons formed the largest percentage of the population and there were no fewer than 297 people with the name in the Reeth union alone. In Durham the greatest concentration was in Teesdale but the name was also well represented in Darlington, Auckland and the city of Durham itself. In the West Riding, the highest totals were in Bradford and Leeds although the name was also firmly established between Skipton and Sedbergh. The numbers and concentrations in Lancashire and Westmorland reflect the spread of the name into those counties.

There were smaller clusters in and around London, as one might expect, and the only real surprise is a group of forty isolated in the Newtown area of Montgomeryshire. An early move into that area by just one Alderson family would explain the name's relative frequency there and the problem invites genealogical investigation. In the meantime it is interesting to note a point made by John and Sheila Rowlands in *The Surnames of Wales* (1996): they commented briefly on a suspected 'plantation' of parts of that county by English families in the late 1500s.

Local historians have long been aware of the remarkable concentration of Alderson in and around Upper Swaledale, and it is surprising that the standard reference works make no mention of its tight-knit distribution in that upland region. Even more surprising is the failure to identify its meaning, for in those few dictionaries where Alderson is listed the derivations offered are most unlikely to be correct. It is a 'filial' name, that is to say it has 'son' as the suffix, and it was established long ago that such names are characteristic of the northern half of the country. On its own that is not enough to account for Alderson's distinctive history and distribution and the key factor is the interpretation of the first element, the personal name which singles it out from many other names in the same category.

Typical filial names are Thompson, Johnson, Robinson and Wilson which are all extremely numerous in Britain and can be seen to derive from the popular first names Thomas, John, Robert and William. We would expect these to have numerous family origins but they cannot be compared directly with Alderson which has a much less transparent meaning. What makes it so distinctive is its derivation from a woman's name rather than a man's. We have several such examples in Yorkshire, including Dyson, prolific in the Colne valley, Tillotson, numerous in Airedale, and Silson, a rare name that originated in Littondale. They derive from Dionisia, Matilda and Cecilia and the evidence suggests that they all had single origins: that inference has already been supported by DNA evidence in the case of Dyson.

The source of Alderson is the more unusual woman's name Aldus, rarely used after *c*.1300. The 'us' ending might be misleading for it seems to link the name with the latinised spellings of male names such as Robertus and Ricardus, forms which were usual in early documents, but the contexts in which Aldus occurs make it clear that we are dealing with a woman's name. Two Yorkshire examples are Aldus de Rilston, the sister of Elias (*c*.1190), and Aldus filia Cristine (1219). It was not until the fourteenth century that surnames with 'son' as a suffix began to stabilise, and by that time Aldus was no longer a popular choice. Even so, the by-names 'filius Alduse' and Alduson occur occasionally in different parts of the county in the 1300s, although none of them has yet been identified as the undisputed source of the surname. One example that occurs close to where the later expansion took place is Thomas filius Alduse, a man who was taxed in Fearby in 1327. The eccentric genealogist Plantagenet-Harrison claimed to have found the name in Keld from the 1390s and it was certainly in that part of Yorkshire that it later ramified successfully.

There is evidence for that ramification in a series of Swaledale wills for the period 1522–1600, edited by Elizabeth Berry. In her introductory remarks she commented on the practice of partible inheritance in Swaledale and the custom is likely to have had some influence on the way surnames expanded in that part of Yorkshire. The wills show that Alderson was prominent in the dale throughout the century and many of the testators had several sons. The family formed a close-knit community and it is noticeable how they served one another as witnesses, supervisors and appraisers. For example, when Richard Alderson of Thorns in Grinton died, in 1559, he referred to a lease that he and Christopher Alderson had of Jeffrey Alderson and four men named Alderson drew up the inventory of his goods.

The family's influence and clannishness is evident in many wills, not just those of close kinsmen. When Bryan Kypling of Angram died, in 1576, one of the supervisors was an Alderson and so were all four witnesses. Prominent among those were Christopher Alderson of 'the Kelde' and Christopher Alderson of Angram, and this repeated use of certain first names helps us to understand why nicknames and by-names would become increasingly necessary. A will of 1580 contains evidence of brothers with the same name, a practice that was more common than genealogists realise. In the will, Agnes Alderson of West Stonesdale made bequests to two sons who were both called John: the second of these was known as Jenkin and she expressed the hope that he would be 'ordred and governed by John his brother' or else forfeit his 'benefytt'.

IN MEMORY OF
CHRISTOPHER ALDERSON ESQ.,
BORN AT ASKRIGG,
WHO DIED DEC. 21. 1810, AGE 82,
AND WHOSE REMAINS ARE DEPOSITED
AT HACKNEY,
IN THE COUNTY OF MIDDLESEX.

HIS HONOUR AS A COMMERCIAL MAN IS UNSULLIED
HIS BEHAVIOUR IN SOCIAL LIFE WAS INTELLIGENT,
AFFABLE AND ENGAGING, TO HIS PIETY AS A CHRISTIAN
THE ALMSHOUSES ERECTED AT GRANGE,
BEAR AN EVINCING PROOF.

AS A TOKEN OF REGARD FOR SO BENEVOLENT A MAN
THIS MONUMENT WAS ERECTED BY HIS NEPHEW
C. A. ALDERSON,
OF WOODHALL PARK,
IN THE YEAR 1819.

SACRED TO THE MEMORY OF
CHRISTOPHER ALDERSON ALDERSON
OF WOODHALL PARK ESQ
WHO DIED AT HIGHWOOD MIDDLESEX
APRIL 22ND 1837
AGED 51.
AND OF MARY HIS WIFE
WHO DEPARTED THIS LIFE
SEPTEMBER 20TH 1825
AGED 36.

Monuments to the Alderson family in Askrigg church. Note the use of Alderson as a first name. (*The author*)

In the hearth tax of 1673 Alderson was such a prolific surname in the region that no fewer than forty-two individuals were taxed in Muker, a territory that covered much of the upper dale. There were six Simons, five Georges and five Williams and all these combinations were recorded in neighbouring parishes. I have Marion Moverley to thank for drawing my attention to an article in the *Wensleydale and Swaledale Almanac* of 1912 in which the author referred to the Aldersons saying that 'almost every individual had an additional name given to him – some of these were characteristic of the mental, personal or physical peculiarity of the owner, others were acquired from some uncommon event ... not a few were occupational and others were place names'. There was evidence too that some were inherited, passed on to a man's offspring through several generations. In Muker, for example, the nicknames 'Knockey' and 'Dick Dack' were borne by several individuals around 1800. The writer of the article signed himself 'Matty Jammie Tom'.

We do not yet know whether it was this expansion in Swaledale that took the surname into Durham or whether it has a separate origin there. Nor is it possible to find an obvious link between the Swaledale family and those Aldersons recorded in different parts of Durham and Yorkshire towards the end of the 1400s. Examples have been noted in Finchale Priory in Durham, and in Hovingham, York and Beverley. Nevertheless it seems certain that the Swaledale family was responsible for much of the ramification noted in the statistics for 1881.

DECLINE AND EXTINCTION

Many of the surnames that we come across in old documents failed to ramify or did not survive into the modern period, and one result of that is that they are largely ignored by family and local historians. Nor do such names usually find a place in surname dictionaries which, for fairly obvious reasons, concern themselves mostly with those that survived in good numbers – what might be termed the 'successful' names. It is a great pity, since some of those lost surnames are of great interest, not just linguistically and genealogically but because the families were for so long part of the fabric of the parish. Perhaps the assumption is that names which became extinct did so early in their history, long before they had time to expand, but that was not always the case. Many have declined in importance over the last two centuries even when the population generally has been on the increase.

A sequence of Tudor subsidy rolls for Craven in the period 1510–47 provides ample evidence of names that were once well established in the Dales but are now either extinct or close to extinction. Typical examples, with the numbers counted in the census of 1881 are: Painley (4); Feaser (6); Beamsley (9) and Danser (20). Others which were once numerous had been lost to the West Riding by 1881. There were no

The Serjeantsons of Hanlith claimed descent from William the Serjeant, an official of Fountains Abbey. The effigy of the serjeant, halberd in hand, is conspicuous in the gable of the modernized hall. (*The author*)

Lawklands, for example, although the variants Lakeland (113) and Lackland (72) survived in Lancashire. The Giggleswick surname Claphamson was extinct but may be the source of Clappinson (12) and the East Riding Clappison (126).

A typical example of a name that failed to ramify is Whittingdale which derives from Whitendale in the Forest of Bowland. From the fourteenth century, examples have been recorded at regular intervals in the parishes along the border with Lancashire, and branches of the family were established in Slaidburn and Thornton in Lonsdale over many generations. Examples in Thornton include: 1522 Richard Whytlyndall; 1629 Robert Whitendale; 1767 William Whittingdale. In 1881 there were just ten people in Britain named Whittingdale, not one of them in Yorkshire but six in Clitheroe: three individuals in Settle had the even rarer spelling Whitendale. Whittingdale survives as the name of a Conservative MP whose Christian names are John Flasby.

A similar story is that of Raingill, another surname from that part of the West Riding. The spelling points to a place-name origin, and the most likely source is a locality named Raingill in the former township of Easington. It formed part of Kirkstall Abbey's estate in Bowland and Adam de Rayngyll is referred to in 1366, in a memorandum in the Coucher Book that related to lands in Slaidburn. The family was an integral part of the community in Slaidburn parish for many centuries but there seem to be no Raingills in Yorkshire now. However, the name survives in Cheshire and sixteen were recorded there in 1881. On the other hand, thousands of people with Ribblesdale connections are likely to have Raingills among their ancestors.

Because the Slaidburn parish registers survive only from 1600 and have important omissions after that, a detailed genealogy of the Raingills is out of the question. In fact the earliest register reference to the family is the marriage entry for George Raingill and Jenet Spenser on 20 November 1600, and the first baptism is that of John Raingill in March 1631. There is no mention of this child's parents but the father may have been Christopher Raingill since he had a daughter Rosamund baptised in 1633. Another member of the family called John Raingill was living at Moor End at that time and he also had a son John, born just three months after Rosamund.

A few testamentary documents for Slaidburn allow us to take the history of the family back a little further. For example, Thomas

Raynegill died intestate in 1580 and the administration of his goods was granted to John Ranegill, his brother. This man may have been the John Rangill of Newton who died in 1595, leaving items to his brother Peter, a son George and an illegitimate daughter Cecile. He also made a bequest to Robert Parker alias Rangill, an illegitimate son of Richard Parker. To complicate the genealogical process further, yet another John Rangill died later that year at Knowlmere and his will shows that he was the father of sons called George and Christopher.

A tax list of 1543 provides us with the names of an earlier generation but offers no real genealogical help. There was nobody with that name taxed in either Easington or Slaidburn but three members of the family were listed in Newton in Bowland. They were Christopher, George and the widow of Peter, bearing first names already encountered in the later wills and registers. These were all adults, so it is probably safe to assume that the family had been living in the parish for some time. The Kirkstall Abbey coucher book mentions Adam de Raingyll in Slaidburn in 1367.

In the seventeenth century the surname continued to be numerically important in Slaidburn, with Christopher and George as favourite first name choices. There were branches of the family living at different times in half a dozen locations, including Moor End, Woodhouse, Wyresdale, Cross and Newton. There were Raingills at Whitehalgh or White Hill House for over a century and Christopher Raingill was living there until his death in 1682. He was succeeded by his brother George who died in 1697 but there were apparently no sons to follow them and this was the beginning of the surname's decline. In fact Henry Raingill, who died at Thornyholme in 1778, may be the last recorded male in the parish, although the surname survived there until 1792 when Alice Raingill was buried.

LINGUISTIC DEVELOPMENT AND ORIGIN

Family historians readily recognise that the spelling of a surname may change from one generation to another and in many cases they are able to identify such variations without too much trouble, as in the case of Metcalfe. On the other hand there are occasional dramatic changes which prove exceptionally difficult to identify. John Broxop of Bolton by Bowland, for example, had a surname in 1543 which became Broscombe in Batley and Birstall, and a dozen or more different forms can be found in other registers. It would be exciting for genealogists if DNA tests could link these different families.

The origin of a Giggleswick surname proved even more difficult to establish since the significant change took place early in its history. Among the earliest entries in the Giggleswick register are: 1559 Edmund Falthropp and 1569 Rowland Fawthrop. The latter is now the usual spelling in Yorkshire and both Fawthorp and Fawthorpe are easily recognised variants. The problem is that it proved difficult for a long time to identify a possible source for the surname since there was no evidence of a place named Falthorpe or Fawthorpe. Fortunately, we can link the reference of 1559 with one in the registry of wills in York over a century earlier, i.e. 1454 John Falthorp of Giggleswick, and this points to a possible connection with a family called 'de Fawelthorpe' which flourished in Broughton, near Skipton, in the fourteenth century. Two poll tax returns for Broughton survive and they confirm the identification, listing Richard de Falthorp in 1377 and Richard de Famelthorp [sic] in 1379. The name is actually an alias for 'de Broughton' on one occasion.

Even so the source remains a mystery for we have no evidence for a place named Favelthorpe. It is likely though to be an unidentified 'thorpe' near Skipton that was associated with the local family called Fawel. Both the Fawels and the de Fawelthorpes feature prominently in a sequence of Broughton deeds that dates from the thirteenth century.

Similarly, Boocock is a surname that demonstrates how difficult it can be for genealogists when a significant change in spelling occurred at an early date. Writers in the past have suggested etymologies for Boocock that are based on its present spelling and in the most recent national dictionaries the name is mistakenly linked with Baud, Balding, Bawcutt and Boulting, among others. No evidence is offered to support such theories and the explanation that it derives either from a Germanic personal name 'Baldo' or was a nickname for a sprightly, cheerful person can be safely ignored.

The reality is that no examples of the spelling Boocock have been located prior to *c*.1600 and evidence in the parish registers shows that it developed as a variant of Bulcock, via Bowcock. The colloquial pronunciation of words such as 'old' and 'soldier' means that even non-linguists are aware that 'l' was vocalised in that way. The spellings used for a family that lived at Knotts in Bowland in the period 1608–30

Bolton Peel, where a family called 'Boocock' lived in the seventeenth century. 'Thomas Bulcocke of the Peele' was in trouble in 1680 for challenging the authority of Mr Pudsey of Bolton Hall (QS1/19/9). (*The author*)

include Bulcock, Bowcocke and Boocock and that development is explicit in the case of Edward Bowcock alias Bulcock of Howgill in 1677.

In earlier centuries the spelling was usually Bulcock. It was one of the most popular surnames in Skipton in the sixteenth century and several members of the family were recorded in the Loan Book of 1522, among them John and Thomas Bulcok. Unfortunately, the editor of the roll failed to recognise the connection with Boocock and he placed all the examples under the head word Bullock in his index. It is true that these two names were sometimes confused in the past but they have distinct origins.

The spelling 'Bulcocke' was still prominent in Skipton in the subsidy roll of 1543 but by 1601, when John Bowcocke of 'the Crosse in Skipton' made his will, the name was clearly in its transitional stage. We can be certain I think that the new spelling reflected the local pronunciation and examples of 'Bulcock' soon became less common in the West Riding. They survived however in Lancashire and Richard McKinley commented on this form of the name, apparently without realising that it was the source of Boocock.

It is less easy to be certain of exactly where the name originated but it can be traced to Colne in the fifteenth century, on the border between Lancashire and Yorkshire, e.g. 1425 John Bulcok of Marsden [now Nelson], a tenant referred to in Farrer's transcriptions of the Clitheroe court rolls. This solitary example does not solve the problem, especially since identical by-names occur well away from that area, e.g. 1301 John Bulekock of Hutton near Whitby. It is most improbable that these names were linked in any way other than by their etymology, but at least they point to 'bull' as the prefix, with 'cock' as a diminutive. Bulcock and Boocock were treated as separate surnames by Reaney but there is no doubt that they share a common origin.

The distribution of Boocock in 1881 accurately reflected its history. The national total was 1,056 with the main concentration (94.5%) in the West Riding and Lancashire, more precisely between Rochdale in the west and Leeds in the east. There were still significant numbers in Skipton and Wharfedale but Bradford and Halifax were by then at the heart of Boocock's expansion. Lancashire was the stronghold of Bulcock, accounting for more than 80 per cent of the national total of 512. The relatively few West Riding Bulcocks were mostly close to the border.

When it can be shown that experienced etymologists make errors it is hardly surprising that historians have also jumped to false conclusions. The story behind the origin of the surname Mangham, as told by Halliwell Sutcliffe, will serve as an example. He was a writer with a romantic streak and it may be that on some occasions this led him to prefer a good story to the more prosaic facts. In his version of the events a shepherd called Simon found a baby boy among the rocks that make Simon's Seat such a distinctive landmark. The bachelor shepherd took the child away with him and sought the help of his fellows in Barden. They each gave part of their earnings to help the boy in his early years and he became known as Simon Amang 'em. According to the author the Amanghams were a scattered family at the time he was writing, but no date is given for when the child was allegedly found.

Simon's Seat, as seen from Percival Hall. The name is recorded on the Jefferys map of 1771 but the identity of Simon remains unknown. The personal name occurs also in Simon Fell and Simon Stone. (*Peter Van Demark*)

It may be that there were no Amanghams at all when *The Striding Dales* was published, for there is no such surname in the British census returns of 1881 and I have never come across it during the more than fifty years that I have worked on Yorkshire records. Not that we should dismiss the story on that account alone for there is no doubt that Mangham was a Dales' surname for several centuries, and Simon was certainly a popular choice for boys in the family. An early example is that of a blacksmith called Simon Mangham whose home was at 'Linton Bridgehead' in 1635. Another Simon Mangham was living in Hebden in 1685.

The origin of Mangham has long intrigued some of those who still bear the name, both in this country and overseas, and much of what I know about it has emerged from their genealogical research. The first well-documented example appears to be a man in Linton in 1588, called Robert, not Simon, so the name has a long history in Wharfe-dale. It has never been common and there were only 219 in 1881: of those more than three-quarters lived in the West Riding, with south

Yorkshire the major 'home'. DNA tests have now proved a direct relationship between Manghams in Yorkshire, Lancashire, California and Hampshire, and their descent from John Mangham of Buckden has been traced by traditional genealogical methods. He was born about 1750.

There are real problems associated with the identification of this surname, which has sometimes been confused with Maugham. That is because 'u' and 'n' are often indistinguishable in early handwriting and some transcribers have made the wrong choice. There has also been genuine confusion with surnames such as Mangall, and Mangan, so researchers have to be more than ordinarily suspicious of what they find in print. Nevertheless, it now seems unlikely that any example earlier than *c.*1580 will be found, and that leaves open the question of Mangham's origin.

The date 1580 certainly seems too late for Robert Mangham of Linton to have taken the name in his own lifetime, so we should consider the possibility that his name is a variant spelling of a better-known surname. If that is what happened the most likely explanation is that Mangham is a contracted form of Manningham, a rare family name that derives from Manningham near Bradford. It was not unusual for the 'ing' in names of this type to be dropped, as in the case of Hemingbrough/Hembrough, Reminton/Remton, and a reference in Bradford to Mangam Felde Syde (1531) shows that the place-name could be pronounced in that way. Although Manningham is now a very rare surname in Britain, it has been closely linked via DNA with Mangum in America, a result that lends support to the linguistic theory. Unfortunately, it has not yet proved possible for genealogists to confirm the link between Mangham and Mangum.

Not all surnames that have -ham as a suffix derive from place-names. Topham has long been recognised as a Yorkshire surname but it has been wrongly said to derive from a place named Topham near Snaith. That might sound the logical explanation even though the early history of the place-name is not well documented but the distribution of the surname and its linguistic evolution point to a quite different origin.

The surname was already numerous by 1672 and the hearth tax records reveal that it belonged mostly to the Dales, especially Wharfedale, although there were good numbers also in Coverdale and Nidderdale and scattered examples in more than forty localities across the county. The major concentrations were in the townships of Hebden, Stonebeck and Caldbergh and in most cases the spellings corresponded to the modern form. Typical of these was Robert Topham of Hebden who paid tax on two hearths. Close to Hebden there were other Tophams, in Appletreewick, Grassington, Hartlington, Hetton, Linton and Kettlewell and a family connection in that part of Wharfedale seems likely. It is there that much of the early evidence can be found.

A sequence of examples from Kettlewell provides evidence of the way in which the name had developed in earlier centuries, e.g. 1379 John Toppan; 1431 Richard Toppan; 1522 Thomas Topham. There is a similar sequence in the parish of Linton where subsidy rolls and the parish registers prove that such spellings continued to alternate into the late seventeenth century. The surname was so common in Hebden at that time that one individual came to be entered in the register under his nickname: the wife of Thomas Topham 'thick' in 1698 was referred to as the widow of Thomas Thick in 1701.

Advertisements from Edmund Bogg's *Wensleydale and the Lower Vale of Yore.*
(*Author's collection*)

The origin remains uncertain although Toppan may be a development of Topping, which can be explained. In 1379, William Toppyng was taxed in Grassington, whilst in Kettlewell three taxpayers were called Toppan or Toppayn – possibly his kinsmen. If the spelling Topping can be trusted it points to a nickname, for 'topping' was a word in everyday use in the fourteenth century: it referred to the forelock or top lock of hair and was also used regularly for animals. In 1558, Elizabeth Nelstrop bequeathed oxen called 'Topping, Broodhead and Brownberd' to her son Henry. It seems that in rural communities, men and animals could have the same kinds of nicknames.

Most families called Topham may share a common origin, for the records of Fountains Abbey show how the surname was ramifying in the Dales through the 1400s. In 1456–58 Thomas and Richard Toppan or Toppam were tenants at Lofthouse; in 1496 Robert Topham was at Hardcastle and William Topham at West Holme House (Fountains Earth). The surname Topping was common in its own right in 1881, especially in Lancashire, so a direct connection with Topham cannot be ruled out. Nevertheless, the by-name was common enough in the northern counties to have given rise to more than one surname, so DNA tests of both Tophams and Toppings might help to solve that problem. Incidentally, the dictionaries explain Topping as the diminutive of an Old English personal name but that is most unlikely.

Assumptions are often made about name origins based on nothing more than guesswork. It was assumed that Topham must derive from a place-name because of its suffix. Similarly, it is often assumed that any surname which ends in -er must have an occupational origin or be a noun of the 'listener' type. Reaney's suggestion for Harker was that it derives from the Middle English verb 'herkien', meaning to listen, and he interpreted it therefore as a nickname for 'an eavesdropper'. A thirteenth-century by-name that he quoted in support of the theory was from a Somerset source and is most unlikely to be connected with the northern surname. Elsewhere, inventive but incorrect suggestions describe it as a short form of Harcourt or a nickname for 'Hawk eye' but many other writers have simply ignored the name even though it is numerous.

In 1881, the total nationally was 3,157 with the majority of these in Yorkshire and adjoining parts of Durham and Lancashire. The most impressive concentration was in Reeth (120) and that is a reflection of the surname's origin in Swaledale. In 1673, Harker was already

Harkers Coaches, January, 2011. The vehicle is parked here in Reeth, no more than a stone's throw from where the surname originated in the fourteenth century.
(*The author*)

expanding in that region and no fewer than sixteen taxpayers in Muker had the name. A century earlier the spelling was significantly different, e.g. 1575 William Harkeye of Birkdale. Other sixteenth-century spellings in Swaledale were Harkay, Arkay and Herkay and these link it to the Swaledale place-name Harker which has exactly the same sequence of spellings. Smith makes no mention of this place-name but it is found as 'Hercay' in a twelfth-century boundary charter and frequently thereafter. The Peacock family lived at Harkerside in the 1500s and it is spelt 'Herkasyde, Harkayside and Arkcasyde in wills that relate to that family. The earliest example of the surname that I have located is: 1366 Thomas Herkay of Arkengarthdale, mentioned in a bundle of deeds published in the *Yorkshire Archaeological Journal*.

Chapter 5

First Names in the Dales

First name studies are usually considered by family historians to be of limited value, so this examination into naming practices in the Dales is designed to outline some of the ways in which distinctive first names can be of help. In *Christian Names in Local and Family History* (2004) I used the poll tax returns of 1377–81 to prepare frequency lists which reflect the popularity of first names right across the country. Significantly, the tables highlight just how few first names were in use in the period 1250–1400, just when many surnames were stabilising, and this clearly has implications for their derivation. That point has been made already with regard to a few surnames derived from female progenitors but some male names were not at all common and they could give rise to surnames which are more distinctive than is generally thought. Distribution patterns can provide a vital clue and Edmond will serve as an example. It was 23rd in order of popularity in 1377–81.

Five centuries later, in 1881, Edmondson ranked as a common surname nationally with a total of 3,461 and yet it was found almost exclusively in Yorkshire (32%) and Lancashire (50%). The statistics show that it was particularly well established in a number of localities, i.e. Burnley, Lancaster and Ulverston in Lancashire; Sedbergh, Settle and Skipton in Yorkshire, all on the western side of the Pennines. These figures may be a surprise to some family historians. The two maps of that distribution make the point even more dramatically, especially when supported by data from earlier periods. The sixteenth-century subsidy rolls for Craven, for example, show how the surname had ramified in Barnoldswick by 1543. In that year fifty-three people were taxed in the village and no fewer than eight were Edmondsons. A possible source is: 1379 John filius Edmundi of Martons Both. It may seem unlikely that Edmondson is a surname with a single family origin but its distribution suggests that most people with the name had their origins on the Yorkshire/Lancashire border.

Oddy also derives from a personal name but one with an even more distinctive history. It is first recorded in Rimington in 1379 when one of the tax payers was called John Odde. This man's descendants can be traced to that part of Ribblesdale over many centuries: Oddie became the preferred spelling of the surname in Lancashire, especially in Clitheroe and Blackburn, whereas the more popular Oddy ramified in Bradford and Leeds. In 1881, their combined totals were 2,419 and again roughly 80 per cent of these were in Yorkshire and Lancashire. The progenitor was almost certainly Hoddi of Gasegill who lived in Rimington in the period 1280–90 and whose unusual first name had a Scandinavian origin. Intriguingly, there are smaller clusters of the surnames in East Anglia and the Orkney Isles, and these raise questions that might be solved by DNA if genealogical methods fail.

The small number of popular first names in that period is important to family historians in another respect. It means that many of the first names with which we are now familiar were rarely used for long periods, certainly from *c.*1300 into the sixteenth and seventeenth centuries. That is true, for example, of Anthony, Brian and Charles for boys, and Frances, Mary and Susan for girls. They would all re-emerge at a later date but their revival might initially be in one place or among a limited number of related families. As a result, some Christian names can be linked immediately with a particular family or a particular parish. Brian, for example, almost always had connections in the fifteenth and sixteenth centuries with the Stapletons, whereas Michael owed its prominence in the same period to a Halifax clothier called Robert Thompson. This man had left Kirkby Malham around the turn of the century and chose to name his son Michael, no doubt because the church in his native village was dedicated to St Michael: in his will he bequeathed 3s 4d 'to the churche . . . of Sanct Michaell in Maladaill'. He referred also to men called Bairstow and Oates with whom he was closely linked socially, and Michael quickly came to be used in their families also.

The key to that localised popularity is the reference that Robert Thompson made in his will to all the children to whom he had been godfather. We know now that when England was a Catholic country it was the godparents who decided what a child should be called, not the parents alone, and the name-giver in those circumstances often used his own first name. As a result one godparent, male or female, could be responsible for the popularity of a Christian name within one

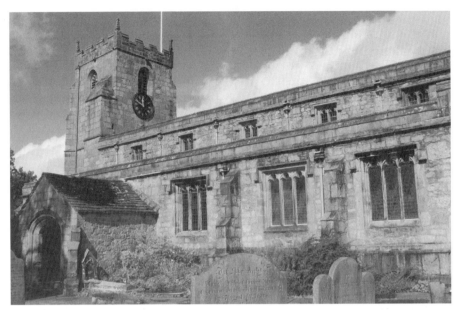

Giggleswick Church, dedicated to St Alkelda. Tradition says that she was a Saxon princess who was strangled by two Danish women *c*.800 and buried at Middleham. Alkelda Browne was married in the church in 1578. (*Peter Van Demark*)

parish or one tight-knit area. These groups of people, linked by the godparent relationship, were known as 'affinities': they were the spiritual families that people belonged to alongside their natural families. There is no doubt that gentlemen in the Tudor period used the practice to ensure that a favoured name became the hall-mark of their affinity, a symbol of their rank and status to go along with their coats of arms. It was a naming practice that would decline in importance after the Dissolution but it continued to influence naming habits as late as 1700. From that time the parents came to play an increasingly important role in name-giving and family historians are familiar with that practice.

In the earlier period and through much of Elizabeth's reign, only the gentry or important clergymen had the power to change naming habits or sanction the introduction of new names, and the choices they made or approved of are often revealing, serving as an insight into religious and political loyalties or the significance that families attached to social status and ancestral origins. It can be fascinating to identify the name-givers of the Tudor period and speculate about their motives, discovering individuals who enriched the national corpus of first names. The studies that follow are intended to illustrate all these points and show how the introduction or revival of first names, and their fluctuating popularity, can be subjects of real value to local and family historians.

SIMON

A close study of the circumstances in which Simon became popular in Swaledale is very revealing. It was a relatively common name everywhere in the fourteenth century, locally and nationally, and four taxpayers in Reeth already had the name in 1301. Only twelve names were more frequent in Yorkshire in 1377–81 and it was possibly at the height of its popularity in those years. The inspiration behind its use was almost certainly the Bible where two apostles had the name, not to mention a brother of Jesus. Nevertheless, its popularity declined in the fifteenth century and by the 1540s it had slipped a long way down the national frequency tables. In general, that decline continued in the period up to 1600, and in the next century it was no longer in regular use. There were several decades when it was no longer in the top fifty.

That was not so in parts of Swaledale where it was used by at least one family in the 1400s and achieved wider popularity over the next two centuries. One consequence of that was that it remained a popular name in some communities well into the twentieth century – against the national trend. Unfortunately, a lack of documentation makes it difficult to discover exactly when and where this local tradition started, and it is only from 1540 that we are on firm ground: in the will of Brian Clarkson of Satron that year one of the supervisors was called Simon Clarkson and there are references in the same period to Simon Bradrigg [Brodrick] of Oxnop (1539) and Simon Blades of Grinton (1544). In Brian Clarkson's will it is clear that he had connections with both those families and the role of the Brodricks may be significant. In a Chancery case of 1562–65, one of the witnesses was Simon Brodrige of Satron, aged seventy-six 'or thereaboutes' which means that he had been baptised back in the late 1480s – the earliest evidence we have.

In the Survey of Lord Wharton's Swaledale estates in 1561 no fewer than seven tenants were called Simon and in two families the name was recorded twice, that is the Brodricks, already noted, and the Aldersons of Angram and Keld. Simon Arkey [Harker] was another notable example. The frequency of Simon in the Alderson family by

1673 has already been commented on but the hearth tax returns for Swaledale show that it was popular more generally: there were three Simon Harkers in Muker alone and other families to use the name were: Brodrick, Hodgson, Lobley, Metcalfe, Milner, Robinson, Spensley and Watson.

We can be fairly sure that the popularity of Simon in that part of Swaledale developed in the Tudor period because of godparent influence and that it initially identified a group of families that was linked spiritually and socially. Such information can help historians and genealogists to identify an affinity within the wider community. After the Dissolution those ties would slowly weaken but Simon continued to be popular and at some stage that must reflect choices made by parents: its frequency in those Swaledale families would certainly have been an indication of kinship by the nineteenth century when so many families left the country.

The work of David Morris has drawn our attention to the importance of this naming habit among Swaledale lead-miners who moved to the United States. One of those was a Simon Alderson who settled at White Oak Springs in 1842; his neighbour Simon Harker had sailed on the *Roscius* in 1839 and went to New Diggings: he would later be joined there by Simon Coates and Simon Brunskill. Another Simon Brunskill settled in Dubuque. The custom survived back in Swaledale too, for William Blades of Dubuque wrote to his friend Simon Cherry in Fremington in 1900. Statistics for the 1881 census reveal that thirty-five men called Simon were then living in the area covered by Reeth Poor Law union, making it the highest concentration in the country. Aysgarth had the second highest concentration. These statistics are evidence of a localised naming practice with a 400–year history.

OSWALD

Other distinctive Christian names have quite different origins and different patterns of popularity. Oswald is a typical example for it was an Old English personal name, destined to fall into obscurity after the Norman Conquest like so many more. It is found in a few twelfth- and thirteenth-century charters but was already out of fashion by 1200 and did not feature in the frequency lists of 1377–81. Unfortunately, there is no agreement among those who compile first-name dictionaries about its later history: Withycombe was aware of Oswald's

Askrigg church, dedicated to St Oswald and the inspiration behind the use of that name among local families, the Metcalfes and the Rouths in particular. (*The author*)

relative popularity in the nineteenth century and that induced her to say that it had never fallen out of use: Hanks and Hodges had a quite different view, commenting on its frequency in the later period as a revival. Their remarks are accurate enough generally, for it was not among the fifty most common English names between 1538 and 1700, but it had a different history in Yorkshire, especially in the Dales.

Although Oswald suffered the same fate after the Conquest as other Old English personal names, it is recorded occasionally in the fourteenth and fifteenth centuries and rather more often in the 1500s. It is unlikely, I believe, that such infrequent references point to a tradition that somehow survived the Norman Conquest and it seems more probable that this sporadic use was inspired by the cult of St Oswald, a great northern saint. Church dedications are likely to have played their part in that and the connection is occasionally implicit, as in the will of William Chamber of Collingham. In 1545 he wrote: 'I bequeathe to my brother Oswalde Chambre my lease of myne officie of the rentes of the late monasterie of sancti Oswaldes': he was referring to Nostell Priory. Dedications to Saint Oswald were particularly popular in the Dales, and responsible, in my opinion, for the use of the name in some Yorkshire communities.

Oswald was certainly popular with some Wensleydale families from the late 1400s, notably the Metcalfes. One Oswald Metcalfe was granted his freedom to trade in York as a grocer and vintner in 1501 and a second witnessed the will of John Whalley of Newhouse in 1570. A third Oswald Metcalfe was taxed in Buckden in 1672. Askrigg church was dedicated to St Oswald and that seems certain to have influenced the choice of the name initially. By the early 1600s, probably within a spiritual affinity, several other Wensleydale families had sons called Oswald, and examples include Oswald Coates of Skellgill (1638) and 'Usewoold' Routh of East Lunds (1658). In 1673, there were seven Oswalds in Wensleydale and quite remarkably they were all in the tax list for Bainbridge. As no fewer than five were called Oswald Routh it is likely that in this family it had become a kinship name, similar to Simon in the Alderson family.

The will of Christopher Routh of Hardraw, in 1667, draws attention to that usage. In it he made bequests to several members of the Metcalfe family and to his brother Oswald; he had his goods appraised by Augustine and Ninian Metcalfe and appointed Oswald Routh of Appersett and Oswald Routh of Hawes to be tutors to his three young children. It is doubtful if we could find a similar group of first names in any other part of the county at that time, possibly in any other part of England, and it emphasises the role played by the Metcalfes as innovative name-givers. Ninian, Augustine and Oswald were all saints' names which were in use in Wensleydale at a time in our history when non-scriptural saints were supposedly quite out of favour. Their popularity in this one region is likely to be an indication of Catholic sympathies, if not among the individuals concerned then among the parents and god-parents who named them. Their choices were certainly distinctive: even if the number of people involved was comparatively small the names occur frequently enough together for us to infer close social and kinship bonds between the families.

It would be wrong to imply that Wensleydale was the only place where Oswald achieved a measure of local popularity, for there are one or two other Yorkshire clusters, notably in other parishes where St Oswald was the church dedication. In Thornton in Lonsdale, the influential Redmayne family used Oswald in the 1500s, followed by the Dicksons and Hudsons. It is worth noting that the curate in

Askrigg until 1593 was Oswald Tatham whose family came from Thornton in Lonsdale. I have not attempted to take the history of Oswald beyond 1700 or look at it more closely across the county but it may be significant that in 1881 Aysgarth Poor Law union had by far the highest concentration of men named Oswald in the country.

CUTHBERT

The history of Cuthbert, another Old English name, has much in common with Oswald but there is an ironic twist in the story. As a first name it can be traced to Durham, for the shrine of St Cuthbert survived in the cathedral and the cult ensured the name's popularity rights across the county and the north-east more generally. However, it arrived in Ribblesdale in the sixteenth century in well-documented circumstances and its subsequent history is remarkable. The first of the name in the parish was probably Sir Cuthbert Musgrave who had been granted the lordship of Knowlmere in Slaidburn *c*.1554, as a reward for his service on the border with Scotland. Ten years later he was at the centre of an acrimonious dispute over seating in the parish church

Knowlmere, Newton in Bowland, 1997. The name had territorial significance, and places such as Farrowfield, Mossthwaite and White Hill House were said to be in Knowlmere. The present villa is probably on the site of the Musgraves' manor house. (*The author*)

and it is likely that he became unpopular with a significant number of local families. It is interesting therefore to look at how his unusual first name fared.

There is no record of Cuthbert as a first name in Slaidburn in any of the population lists that cover the period 1379–1547 but it later became a favourite choice in the Hayhurst family. The earliest entries in the Slaidburn register date only from April 1600 and Cuthbert Hairst or Hayhurst had a daughter baptised in August that year. He is likely to have been the Cuthbert Hairste mentioned in his father's will in 1586 and he would probably have been named ten or fifteen years earlier. Elsewhere, the Hayhurst family was said to be of Knowlmere so the inference is that Cuthbert Musgrave had been the boy's godfather. It was the starting point of a long tradition and there are references to a succession of men named Cuthbert Hayhurst in the Slaidburn parish register. That lasted until at least May 1767 when Cuthbert Hayhurst was still living at Graydale. The name had little influence in the parish outside the Hayhurst family although Cuthbert Guy was living at Fair Hill in 1614 and Cuthbert Cock of Newton was baptised in 1737. These choices may well indicate a relationship with the Hayhursts.

The irony is that the name really came to prominence in a branch of the family that embraced the Quaker faith and there are frequent references to Cuthbert Hayhurst and Cuthbert Hayhurst, junior, in the Quarter Sessions records. In 1671, for example, Cuthbert Hayhurst of 'Knowmear in Newton, yeoman' was 'convicted for beinge at a Conventickle ... at the house of Thomas Wiglesworth of Skelshay'. More seriously, the same man or his namesake had been indicted earlier 'for breakinge of the peace upon the Lord's day in the Church of Slaidburn, to the disturbance of the Congregation'. The family had a troubled time in the parish and finally, in 1682, Cuthbert Hayhurst emigrated with his family to Pennsylvania, probably on a ship named the *Lamb*. They were just one family among many that made the move from Ribblesdale.

This group of Quakers was discussed at length by George McCracken who published a pedigree of the American Hayhursts. This takes their history up to the end of the eighteenth century and includes the name of a Cuthbert Hayhurst who died there in the 1790s, by which time the tradition was already more than two centuries old. In Britain the use of Cuthbert remained very much a north-country custom and it was obviously still influencing the statistics in 1881. In

An old doorhead at Bordley. The date and the initials point to Cuthbert Wade of Kilnsey Hall whose family held property there. He owed his first name to a connection with the Withams, a family with North Riding connections, and it passed from the Wades to the Allansons of Lancashire. (*The author*)

that year Durham and Northumberland were the two counties with the greatest number of men called Cuthbert and the concentration there was exceptional.

LEONARD

It can be worthwhile to pursue the history of almost any uncommon first name in the Tudor period, and church dedications, as I have said, can be a vital clue. The few women called Alkelda that I have come across lived in Giggleswick where the dedication is to St Alkelda: the Ricarys were from Aberford where the dedication is to St Ricarius, an even more obscure name. The practice can be observed even in the case of more widely-used saints' names, such as Leonard. This was exceptionally rare in Yorkshire in the thirteenth and fourteenth centuries and it remained uncommon generally until at least 1700. Throughout that period it was never among the top twenty male names in frequency lists and in the seventeenth century was often out of the top fifty. Nevertheless, there were several districts in the Dales where it was relatively popular for short periods and these groups raise interesting questions for family historians.

The most striking example is in Lindley, near Otley. In 1535 the name featured there four times in a muster roll of just sixteen men, i.e. Leonard Crokbayn, Leonard Cokman, Leonard Pauson and Leonard Turnour. There were more examples close by in Beamsley and New Hall, i.e. Leonard Bayn, Leonard Hamlyng and Leonard Lewty. These numbers assume particular significance when a comparison is made with other communities. In a subsidy roll of 1543, there was not a single Leonard among the ninety-five men named in Skipton, nor was anybody called Leonard in the parishes of Keighley and Kildwick where 277 men were listed.

Despite that, Lindley was not the only place where Leonard was popular in that period for there was a second group a dozen miles away to the south-east in Aberford. At least three men named Leonard had children baptised there between 1540 and 1550 and a further ten children were given the name before 1580. Leonard was actually the sixth most popular boys' name in the parish at that time, more frequent than such traditional names as Henry, Roger and Edward. It is evident that the children in both places would have been baptised in the early part of the century and that they represented a high proportion of what were small communities.

The circumstances in which the name had been revived in that area and its subsequent rapid expansion can be traced, I believe, to the marriage of Robert Mauleverer and Joan Vavasour in *c.*1470. When Sir Henry Vavasour made his will, in 1499, he asked to be buried in 'the chapell of Seint Leonard in Hesilwood' and dedicated his 'mortuary' to the use of the chantry. His eldest son had the name Leonard and subsequently three Mauleverer boys were also given the name. One Leonard Mauleverer who died in 1542 made small bequests to his godsons Leonard Carleton and Leonard Thomson. It is worth noting that one of the Aberford tenants referred to above was called Leonard Thomson and that the Mauleverers had an estate in Beamsley, where Leonard Bayn was living in 1535.

That suggests, but does not prove, a way in which Leonard may have been revived in lower Wharfedale although it does not explain why so many men in the Lindley muster roll were called Leonard in 1535. The key to that may be an affinity which included three gentry families, all with children named Leonard, i.e. the Lindleys who held the manor of Lindley, the Gascoignes and the Beckwiths. Leonard Gascoigne was one of the children baptised in Aberford in 1563 and Leonard Lindley, chaplain, was named in the will of Thomas Lindley in 1524. It is quite possible that he had acted as godfather to the men listed in the muster roll.

However, the connection with the prolific Beckwith family is potentially more interesting. They derived their surname from Beckwithshaw near Harrogate, and Sir Leonard Beckwith came to enjoy great status in the county. Having made a fortune out of land-dealing, he rose to the level of gentleman and was buried in York Minster in 1555. Later generations of Beckwiths used the same first name and it occurs right through the rolls of the Freemen of York, from Leonard Bekwith who was a merchant in 1568 to Leonard Beckwith who was a brewer and scrivener in 1740. For the Beckwiths the name Leonard clearly enjoyed a certain prestige and it was passed from one generation to another, outlasting the original affinity and reminding family members of an illustrious forebear.

Of course the Vavasours are unlikely to have been the only West Riding family to revive the use of Leonard or even the first, and there is evidence of a similar tradition in other parts of Yorkshire. In Thornton in Lonsdale, for example, the name Leonard Tatham occurred consistently in the period 1589–1799, and there were other Leonards in

The chapel of St Leonard, Hazlewood, built by Sir William Vavasour in the late thirteenth century. In 1483, Mr Leonard Vavasour became rector of Addingham and was ordained acolyte at York the following year. The drawing was done by Percy Robinson for Edmund Bogg's *A Thousand Miles in Wharfedale*. (*Author's collection*)

Dent in the seventeenth century. The re-emergence of the name must go back to the middle years of the fifteenth century or even earlier for I have noted several examples of adults with the name in York in 1470–80. One of those was Leonard Helton, a senior priest in York Minster. When he died in 1480 he made a bequest to St Leonard's, the great York hospital.

PERCIVAL

The Lindleys of Lindley are likely to have been responsible also for the popularity in Wharfedale of Percival, not the name of a saint but one drawn from the medieval romances. A few such names were in use by the late fourteenth century although they were by no means popular. Among those taken from the Arthurian cycle were Percival,

Gawain and Tristram, whilst the legends associated with Charlemagne inspired the use of Roland and Oliver. The origin and etymology of such names is often uncertain and Percival falls into that category. It is said to have been coined by Crestien de Troyes for the hero of his poem of that name, towards the end of the twelfth century, and it may be a re-modelling of an older name. On the face of it the meaning is literally 'pierce – vale', a type of name that was quite common in France.

The first person in Yorkshire known to have borne the name was Percival Pensax, a wealthy resident of Beckwithshaw in 1379. He was a neighbour of the Lindleys and possibly related to the family, for they provide several of the examples found in the 1400s: Bernard Jennings quoted from the court rolls of Bilton with Harrogate where he noted that Percival Lyndley held land in 1457; in 1475 Perceval Lyndley witnessed a land deed for Pannal and in 1549 Parcevall Lyndley, gentleman, made his will. It remained a popular family name into the seventeenth century at least and it almost certainly explains the later frequency of Percival in that part of the dale at a lower social level. The muster roll in which Leonard was so prominent includes five other examples of Percival, used by families named Wade, Duffield, Jenkinson, Foster and Hawksworth. Unlike Leonard its popularity there was not short-lived and there are examples in the neighbourhood over subsequent generations, some of them clearly reflecting a local pronunciation, e.g. 1672 Parsibell Foster who was taxed in Leathley in 1672.

There were one or two other regions in the county where Percival became relatively popular in the 1500s but such local concentrations are easily missed in the national statistics. Their identification is there-fore a task that local and family historians might undertake, for such groups can throw new light on a number of topics. No attempt has yet been made to assess the long term influence of the godparents on naming patterns but it is noticeable that Percival was still more common in the West Riding in 1881 than in most other counties. Indeed, there was still a significant cluster in the Knaresborough area.

LANCELOT

Lancelot, like Cuthbert, was a name that was revived outside York-shire but came to play an important role in the Dales. Like most Arthurian first names it has a disputed etymology and it was not a popular name nationally. Nevertheless, its frequency in the north-west of the country stands out from the sixteenth century, at a time when it was missing from the national frequency lists, including those for Yorkshire. One clue to its importance is a rental for Ravenstonedale in 1541 in which no fewer than six tenants had the name. A further clue is in the surnames of the men who had been given the name in the fifteenth century, that is Lancelot Threlkeld (1472), Lancelot Lowther (1487), Lancelot Hutton (1490) and Lancelot Wharton (1511). All these men were gentlemen and they were all from what is now Cumbria. It is a practice that may have had its origins in the Neville family, for they certainly used Lancelot as a first name, but I have been unable to find enough evidence to be sure.

Nevertheless, the natural and spiritual connections between these men and other great northern families are often hinted at and occasionally explicit, as in the case of Lancelot Threlkeld. In 1485, Henry Percy, Earl of Northumberland, referred in his will to several feoffees, among them Lancelot Threlkeld, esquire: in 1490 Lancelot Hutton of Hutton in Cumberland spoke of Lancelot Threlkeld as his 'gossip', that is his 'god sib or relation', a term that confirmed their spiritual kinship. The Yorkshire gentleman Lancelot Stapleton was so called because his mother was Lancelot Threlkeld's daughter. When he died childless, in 1538, he bequeathed 40s to his godson Lancelot Conyers. In his wife's will (1545) there were bequests to Lancelot Brown, Lancelot Fox and Lancelot Knapton.

This gentry network would eventually help to establish the name in a number of scattered Yorkshire communities but there is evidence through the sixteenth century that it had increased its popularity in the Dales, if only for a short time, e.g. 1552 Lancelot Frankland of Halton Gill; 1579 Lancelot Nesfield of Flasby; 1591 Lancelot Dowbiggin of Bentham; 1605 Lancelot Raikes of Kirkby Malham. Other Lancelots have already been referred to in earlier chapters.

GAWIN

Unusual first names are clearly of interest to genealogists but their value can go further than might be suspected, helping to confirm identities or relationships in a more subtle way. The colloquial pronunciation of Hayhurst, for example, produced the spellings Hairst and Haste, both of which survive. It is the first name that confirms the identification. Equally confusing is the assumption by some clerks that

Hairst was really Hirst which is prolific in its own right. That mistake only came to light because Cuthbert was so distinctive. On the other hand, a rare first name can pose its own problems of identification, like the mysterious and apparently unique Guard – the name of a Bainbridge man called Bywell in 1673. In this case his surname was uncommon enough to help solve the problem. Cross reference with other Yorkshire sources provided evidence of men named Gaudyng, Gaudean and Gawden in the period 1554 to 1667, all seen as possible links with 'Guard'. They turn out to be variants of Gawin or Gawain, the name of one of the Knights of the Round Table. Gawdwin Spence of Carlton in Coverdale was a regular juror at Richmond in the early 1600s and was alternatively known as Gawin. Gawyne Bywell was an Askrigg man in the 1590s and the inference is that Guard' Bywell inherited that name. Gawin is usually said to have survived only in Scotland after the sixteenth century, giving us more recently the revived Gavin, but there were Gawins in north Yorkshire over several centuries.

REGIONAL DIFFERENCES

In the period up to the Dissolution it was gentry families who were responsible for changing naming practices and introducing new names into the national corpus, and sometimes these names achieved local popularity via the godparents. Occasionally, a name that had fallen completely out of fashion was deliberately revived in order to empha-sise a family's ancient lineage, and impress less exalted neighbours. I suspect that was the motive of the Arthingtons who revived the Norman name Serle in the sixteenth century: it had previously featured in their twelfth-century charters. It was very soon transformed into Cyril, no doubt by association with St Cyril. The Arthingtons were notorious Catholic recusants and that may have influenced its remoti-vation. Similarly the Vavasours revived the family's use of Mauger, another Norman name, but this was a choice that spread to their tenants and kinsmen, unlike Cyril which remained very uncommon. Mauger, or Major as it was popularly spelt, was used by a score of families in lower Wharfedale as late as the nineteenth century, by which time Major as a military title was emerging as a first name in its own right. It was also in the sixteenth century that surnames came into use as first names, another gentry practice that initially emphasised family connections and lineage. A striking example in the Dales was

Markenfield Hall: a fortified manor house built by the Markenfields in the early 1300s. When Sir Thomas Markenfield named his son and heir Ninian *c.*1460, he started a local tradition that lasted for centuries. Trinian is the Gaelic form of Ninian and the use of both in Wensleydale indicates familiarity with Ninian's shrine in Scotland. (*The author*)

Tempest which was used for boys in the Slinger family for centuries and passed from them to the Coulthursts of Gargrave, as a girl's name.

After the Dissolution, as the role of the godparents declined in importance, local ministers and parents could play a more important role as name-givers and their influence can be traced in a wide variety of documents. In order to illustrate that development I have compiled frequency lists for male names in different parts of the northern dales, using the hearth tax returns of 1673. This allows the practices of neighbouring communities to be studied in some detail and the lists can be compared with the national lists and those from other parts of the Pennines.

One major point to emerge from this comparison is the lack of importance that names from the Old Testament had in most of the northern dales. Few names in this category had been popular in

England in the Middle Ages, but they had been introduced or reintroduced in some Pennine parishes in the mid-1500s by families with Puritan sympathies. In the Calder valley, for example, outside the Dales area, Abraham and Jonas were in the top ten in 1672, followed by Joseph, David, Jonathan, Samuel, Nathaniel, Daniel, Isaac and Jeremiah. All these were among the thirty most popular names. Nationally, Old Testament names had much less importance, although Samuel and Joseph were both in the top twelve and several others found a place in the top thirty, i.e. Daniel, Joshua, Abraham, Nathaniel and Benjamin. By contrast only Adam and Daniel were recorded in Swaledale and Abraham in Wensleydale.

Moreover, the inclusion of Adam here could be misleading since it was not one of the names revived by Puritans but a survivor from a much older tradition. From the 1200s it was always more common in parts of north-west England than it was generally. Closer scrutiny reveals that Adam was used by four Muker families in 1673, the Aldersons, Harkers, Coateses and Proctors, and it had a long history in the first three of these. Over all, the Swaledale names were actually far more traditional than those in the Calder valley, and the influence of a few families is particularly noticeable. The popularity of Simon has already been discussed but Jeffrey was a survival similar to Adam and it owed its limited popularity to a different group of families, i.e. Metcalfe, Raw, Wharton, Wensley and Tunstall (2).

Mention was made earlier of the influence that the prolific Metcalfe family appear to have had on naming practices in Wensleydale, and the lists of 1673 emphasise that point: among the names recorded that year were several that were not in the top fifty nationally, i.e. Austin, Brian, Jeffrey, Lionel, Percival, Simon and Trinian. Each one of these is worth investigation but just two will be mentioned here. Augustine, better known in the colloquial form Austin, may have been inspired by the first Archbishop of Canterbury or by the St Augustine whose monastic rule gave rise to the so-called Austin Friars. It had fallen from popularity by the late 1300s and was still generally uncommon in 1673. Nevertheless, it was a frequent choice in the Metcalfe family from the late 1500s: in 1599, for example, Augustin Metcalf of Coverhamside was granted licence to marry Mabel Dinsdale of Gale in Askrigg; in 1655 Augustine Metcalfe of Cotterdale made bequests to his grandson Augustine and also to Augustine Parkin, another Wensleydale man taxed in 1673.

Burnsall church is dedicated to St Wilfrid and this window links him with
Lindisfarne and York. A major centre of his cult was Ripon where he was buried and
the personal name enjoyed some popularity in Yorkshire from the late 1400s. It was
often spelt Wilfrey in earlier centuries. (*The author*)

Perhaps the most unexpected name in the list is Trinian, borne by two Metcalfes in 1673 and by seven or eight other local families at least. The inspiration may have been St Trinian's near Richmond, the seat of a family called Robinson in the 1600s. Trinian was actually a variant of Ninian, the name of a fifth-century saint, and occasionally the alias was explicit, e.g. 1611 Ninian alias Trinian Smithson of Newton. In 1577, Nynyand Metcalf had been named in the will of Thomas Metcalfe of Fossdale and in 1686 Trinjan Metcaffe was an appraiser of the goods of John Metcalfe of Hardraw. The diminutives Ninny and Trinny were also used.

In conclusion it should be emphasised that the names looked at here are only examples. There are numerous other first names in the Dales that repay investigation, e.g. Giles, Marmaduke, Miles, Ranald or Reynold, Roland, Solomon, Wilfrid or Wilfrey and Vincent. Even some of the more popular names such as Anthony and Peter have distinctive local associations. The giving of a first name was a deliberate and thoughtful act and this makes the study of their frequency and use a vital tool for family historians.

Chapter 6

Migration

A great deal has been written about the successful expansion of Yorkshire surnames and the continuity of families in those parts of the county where they originated, and it is certainly true that many names can still be found in good numbers close to where they were first recorded over 600 years ago. Less has been said about the many surnames that survived or expanded well away from their point of origin, either in other parts of the county, in England more generally, or even overseas. The truth is that the story of the migrant is much more difficult to tell, for his absence may not be noted by the local historian and his origins can be difficult to trace, even by dedicated genealogists.

The story of the Hartlington family is one illustration of a name that was prominent in the Dales for generations and then apparently disappeared without trace. As a by-name it is found in the early records of Furness Abbey, starting with William de Hertlington in *c.*1200: an inquisition post mortem places a second William de Hertlington in Hartlington in 1279 and Henry de Hartelyngton was taxed there just a century later. A Bolton Priory rental of 1473 has William and Henry Hartlyngton as tenants in Appletreewick and Malham. These are just a few of numerous early references to the family but by the sixteenth century the surname was scarce, certainly in the Dales, and tax lists for the period 1510–47 seem to contain one example only, that of Hugh Hartlington of Newton in Slaidburn parish in 1524. Actually, a closer look at the lists for the individual townships guides us to two later entries for the same person: 1525 Hugh Hurlton of Newton and 1543 Hugh Hurlenton of Newton. Family historians will note the significant spelling change and the failure of the index to identify the connection.

Evidence from the Slaidburn register takes the story of this rare surname into the next century with a single reference in 1638 to William, an illegitimate son of Elizabeth Hartlington. On the other hand there are many more references there to the variant spelling found in

1525–43 and these confirm that the family survived in Slaidburn into the early 1700s. Typical examples are: 1634 Hugh Hurlington or Hurtlingeton of Brunghill Moor and 1718 John Hurlington of Slaidburn, a tailor. The trail appears to end with the burial of this John Hurlington for the name is subsequently absent from the registers. The Slaidburn wills that have been transcribed by Chris Spencer, together with entries in the Slaidburn court rolls, help the genealogist to reconstruct much of the family's history in the earlier period but otherwise the evidence points to the surname's eventual extinction *c.*1718, especially as the West Riding hearth tax returns for 1672 contain no references to either Hartlington or Hurlington.

It was a letter from Mr Edwin Horlington of Walton on the Naze in Essex that alerted me to the surname's survival. He had traced his own descent in the south of England from a man called John Horlington who lived in Holborn in the early 1700s and had served as a witness in a Chancery case. Further research showed that he had previously used the spelling Hurlington but 'Horlington' was the preferred form thereafter. He seems likely to have been the John Hurlington baptised in Slaidburn in 1696.

Few lessons can be learned from the movement of one man to London in the early eighteenth century but the distribution of surnames generally is not as random as might be thought and certain patterns are discernible. Social and economic circumstances have played their part in that as have the available routes of communication. One illustration of that is that surnames which originated on the western flanks of the Yorkshire Pennines may now be more common in parts of Lancashire than they are in Yorkshire. The history of Dowbiggin, an uncommon name which derives from the hamlet of Dowbiggin in Sedbergh, will serve as an example. Adam de Doubiging witnessed a Sedbergh deed in 1321 and examples of the name are then recorded in that part of Yorkshire at regular intervals, right up to the census of 1881. On the other hand it was found principally in Lancashire by that time with small but significant groups in Liverpool, Preston and Lancaster. Together these accounted for about 60 per cent of the national total. Other members of the family were in Kendal and Cumberland. Richard McKinley comments on the presence of the surname in Lancashire from the seventeenth century.

Yorkshire families are known to have moved into that region as early as the fourteenth century. The following by-names or surnames all occur in the Lonsdale section of the Lancashire poll tax returns of 1379: Austwick, Bland, Clapham, Elslack, Hubberholme, Ingleton, Paythorne, Rathmell, Rimington, Stainforth and Twisleton. Not all these survived but one or two certainly did and the list is evidence of how mobile families were by that time. Clearly such a move could affect a name's eventual distribution. It would be interesting, for example, to discover when the first Armitstead moved into Lancashire, for the surname is more numerous there now than it is in Yorkshire. The main variations are Armstead, Armistead and Armitstead and the 1881 statistics illustrate the expansion of all three in places such as Blackburn, Burnley, Bury, Lancaster and Preston. Together the two counties account for approximately 70 per cent of the national total of 1,160, but Lancashire's share is 42 per cent. The surname derives from Armitstead in Giggleswick and it was prominent there for centuries. The spelling Armitstead was rare in 1881 but the total of 132 included thirty-eight in Kendal.

Surnames which derive from distinctive place-names can be relatively easy to trace but that is seldom true of names in other categories. Gregson appears to be straightforward for it clearly derives from a pet form of Gregory. On the other hand this was a very uncommon first name in the late 1300s when the surname became hereditary. The poll tax returns of 1379 contain details that seem certain to relate to its origin on the border between Yorkshire and Lancashire: in the Lonsdale region of Lancashire there were two families named Gregson and one named Gregoryson; in Yorkshire there were four more Gregsons close by in Austwick and Clapham and Joan Gregdoghter in Thornton in Lonsdale – a Yorkshire village. The identity of the progenitor is an intriguing problem for local historians, especially as Gregory was itself a prolific Lancashire surname. In 1881, Gregson was also common with a national total of 4,145: of these two thirds were in Lancashire, with high concentrations in Preston and Blackburn, whereas Yorkshire had only 583, a small total by comparison.

It would be wrong to imply that such a distribution pattern was in any way unusual. The truth is that the dispersal of such names by 1881 was to be expected. Migration from Yorkshire into Lancashire, or the other way around, was often over a relatively short distance, sometimes into a neighbouring parish. That mobility poses a problem for the family historian but it is made more difficult because we store our archives in County record offices. The arbitrary changes to the county boundaries in 1974 made research into places such as Dent and Slaidburn even more complicated.

LINGUISTIC VARIATIONS

Another aspect of the subject is that migration could lead to the preservation of archaic spellings. In regions where surnames had a long history, often close to the place of origin, there eventually developed a perception of what the 'correct' form should be and the more unusual variations were progressively eliminated. That was not always the case when the name was being recorded well away from its source.

If we return for a moment to Dowbiggin, the census returns show that by 1881 Dowbikin, Dowbekin and Dowbakin were all Lancashire surnames. On the other hand these developed from spellings that had once been traditional in Yorkshire, e.g. 1596 Margaret Dowbikin, Clapham; 1652 Lancelot Dobikin, Ingleton. In the hearth tax of 1672 the only example of the surname in the West Riding was Lancelot Dowbikin of Ingleton. There can be no doubt that the present spelling Dowbiggin has stabilised more recently, probably under the influence of the place-name.

Vernacular spellings were sometimes preserved when a name moved away from where it was well known and migration also exposed it to regional interpretation. Suffixes were particularly vulnerable to change and the variations were not necessarily predictable linguistically: a 'difficult' element like -thwaite might finish up as -field, -foot, -well, -white or -wood. One relevant example is Thistlewood for Thistlethwaite, implicit in the Arncliffe register, i.e. 1671–74 John Thiselwhit or Thiselwod of Hawkswick. Similarly, Kettlewood may be a variant of Kettlewell. One of the first examples on record is John Kettlewood of Settrington who made his will in 1546: a second John Kettlewood married Agnes Jackson there in 1563 and a third became a leaseholder in 1588. When this man died, in 1598, he left the premises to his widow and after her death to his children Lawrence, Matthew and John.

There is a clue to the name's origin in the records of Ripon Grammar School. In 1567, a former master of the school was accused of being a Papist – 'a misliker of Christe's religion nowe established'. He was said to 'lurk' about Ripon and was 'commonlie harboured at the howse of one Robert Kettlewood'. The editor of the document thought that Kettlewood was probably a mistake for Kettlewell but if the man was protecting a known papist it seems more likely that he shared his beliefs and preferred the spelling Kettlewood because it might obscure his origins and help him to avoid detection. Similar cases are well documented. Significantly, the manor of Settrington was held at that time by the Bigod family, who also owned property in Swaledale close to where a branch of the Kettlewell family was living. In the 1881 census, just twenty-three Kettlewoods were counted, all but two of them in Yorkshire, and Pocklington in the East Riding was their main 'home'.

GROUP MIGRATION

This possible link between Settrington and Swaledale draws attention to an early phase of migration, and it is the dale's distinctive surnames that help to tell the story. One of the finest sources of information for Swaledale surnames is Elizabeth Berry's *Swaledale Wills and Inventories* (1998) and if it is studied in conjunction with the published registers for Grinton it is soon clear which families had a long history in the dale. Names which derive quite obviously from local place-names include Fothergill, Harker and Blades, whilst Tiplady stands out as a distinctive local nickname. The fact that all four of these were established in Settrington by 1560–70 is intriguing, for this was an unlikely destination on the face of it. Settrington is an East Riding township at the northern foot of the Wolds, more than fifty miles to the south-east. Nevertheless, the evidence for such a group migration is compelling.

The origin of Harker and its spelling history have already been discussed and early examples from the Settrington registers reflect that development: the burial of Widow Harkey took place in 1568 and John Harke married Agnes Barker in the same year: Miles Harker had a son, Ralph, baptised in 1562. In a Settrington survey of 1599, Ralph Harker was the tenant of land that had been leased to his father Miles in 1570, by the Earl and Countess of Lennox.

The less well-known surname Blades derives from the hamlet of Blades near Feetham: William de Blades was taxed at Reeth in 1301 and John Bladdes was living at Crackpot in 1540. Other branches of this family were established at Grinton and Skelton. Blades, like Harker, is a place-name that was not included in Smith's *Place-Names of the North Riding* and these omissions help to explain why writers have failed to identify the origins of the surnames. It is known that Francis Blaides was resident in Settrington in the 1570s and that he

The ornate Jacobean pulpit in Grinton church. It would have been familiar to many of the Swaledale families who emigrated to America but not to those who moved to Settrington in the sixteenth century. (*The author*)

served as the deputy bailiff of the manor, living for a time in the manor house.

In the Settrington survey of 1599 one of the farms was in the tenancy of William and James Fothergill. They had inherited it from their father William and before that it had belonged to Rowland Fothergill, their grandfather. Rowland's name is one of the first in the Settrington registers which survive from 1559. The origin of this surname is less straightforward but it may derive from an unidentified site in Mallerstang, just over the border with Westmorland: John de Fothergall was taxed at Kirkby Stephen in 1379. It may be worth noting though that in 1301 Robert de Fagardgill was taxed in Arkengarthdale, taking his by-name from the settlement of Faggergill.

What can be said with certainty is that the Fothergill family had strong connections with Ravenstonedale and Mallerstang, and the surname ramified strongly in that region. A rental of 1541 for Ravenstonedale, printed in an old history of the area, has sixteen tenants with the surname and among these were two called Rowland, the first name found in Settrington. Rowland was not a common name generally at that time. In Swaledale, the family had land in Birkdale, and Richard Fuddergill witnessed the will of James Carter of Kearton in 1560.

The final name for consideration is Tiplady, usually said to have originated as a nickname for a philanderer. As a by-name, not neces-sarily hereditary that is, it is on record in more than one North Riding village in the 1300s and the surname later became prominent both in Swaledale and Cleveland: it is not known if the two groups had any family connection. It cannot be assumed therefore that the Settrington freeholder John Tiplady (1563) had his origins in the Dales but it seems likely. Branches of the family there had property in Marrick and Grinton, not very far from Aysgarth where Thomas Typledy was taxed in 1377.

These are by no means the only surnames common to both Swaledale and Settrington in the 1500s, and at least twenty more could be listed. They include Milner, Peacock, Fryer, Banks and Waller, as well as some which are more common generally, i.e. Harrison, Jefferson, Taylor and Thompson. In such cases it would be extremely difficult to prove a link with Swaledale. A few others stand out as surnames more usually associated with the Dales than with the Malton area, e.g. Colby, Hebblethwaite and Teesdale. Large or small, a movement of families from Swaledale to Settrington seems certain to have taken place in the early 1500s and that makes the possible role of the Bigod family worth investigating. Their estate included Settrington and a half share of Healaugh in Swaledale.

The link may be with Sir Francis Bigod who was executed in 1537 for the part he played in the Pilgrimage of Grace. In January of that year he raised a rebellion designed to defend the north against royal retribution and is said to have visited Healaugh where he encouraged his tenants to rise in revolt. It can hardly be a coincidence that Francis Blaides of Settrington bore that first name, for he christened his son Bygod in 1591. Perhaps the migration of these Dales' families had something to do with the rebellion.

LEGEND AND FACT

Of course it is dangerous to speculate, for that is what lies behind so many family traditions and legends. Occasionally, though, a legend can be tested against the known facts. Among the many memorable stories told by Ella Pontefract and Marie Hartley is a late chapter in the history of a family called Ibbotson who were well-known horse-dealers in Wharfedale. The tale that captures the imagination is that of Jamie Ibbotson who died in 1926, the last of the Threshfield besom-makers. Halliwell Sutcliffe was almost certainly talking about this family, although he did not name them, when he wrote about the besom-maker's house by the beck in Threshfield and recounted the fascinating conversations that the two men had together.

Particularly interesting is the picture we are given of a man who gathered all that he needed for his craft in the surrounding country-side: stems of heather from the moor, handles from the hazel coppice and bark from local ash trees for the bands that were used to tie the bundles together. Perhaps the one item in the Ibbotsons' story that can be looked at more carefully is the romantic family tradition that their ancestors had come south from the Scottish Borders in the early 1600s, soon after the union of the Scottish and English thrones. We are told that earlier generations had been cattle-rangers and moss-troopers before they settled in Threshfield as besom-makers. We can certainly find information that relates to those questions in family history sources.

Ibbotson was actually a well-established surname in Wharfedale from long before 1600, although the surname in that early period was

A quiet corner of Threshfield, once the centre of the besom-making industry in Wharfedale. The Ibbotsons were the last family so employed. (*The author*)

quite often spelt Ebotson. James Ibbotson was buried at Linton in 1587 and John and Alexander Ebotson were taxed in Threshfield as early as 1543: their contemporaries included John and Leonard Ibotson of Kettlewell. A generation before that, in 1522, John and James Ebotson of Kettlewell were tenants of Lord Conyers. Another Leonard Ebotson was listed in Grassington in c.1510, as a bowman in the so-called muster roll for Flodden. By inference this takes the history of the surname back into the late 1400s. The parish registers and hearth taxes provide evidence of a surname that continued to be prominent in Wharfedale through the 1600s, not only in Threshfield, Grassington and Kettlewell, but also in Cracoe, Hebden and Rylstone, and something of the status of these families emerges from other sources. Wills, for example, show that Anthony Ibotson of Knott Green in Hebden was a 'husbandman' (1674), whilst Richard Ibbotson of Rylstone was a yeoman (1673). In 1685, James Ibbotson of Threshfield, along with his wife and five children, was awarded 2s relief in a benefaction to the poor.

The statistics show that Ibbotson was overwhelmingly a Yorkshire surname in 1881. Of 2,059 Ibbotsons listed, no fewer than 1,403 resided in the West Riding, almost 70 per cent, and most of the remainder were in other parts of Yorkshire or in neighbouring counties such as Lancashire and Durham. There were two Ibbotsons in Cumberland, just one in Northumberland and three in the whole of Scotland. The name was most prolific in an area to the north of Sheffield, where its history is well documented from the fourteenth century. Of course very little of this evidence is strictly genealogical, but it casts doubt on the story that the Ibbotsons moved south from the Scottish Borders.

There is no suggestion of a link between the Ibbotsons in Wharfedale and those in south Yorkshire. The derivation is from the popular woman's name Isabel, via the diminutives Ebbot or Ibbot and the evidence makes it clear that the surname had more than one origin in the county. In the poll tax of 1379 the by-name was recorded in a dozen West Riding villages, including Newall in Otley. In Cawthorne, William Souter and his wife Ibot were listed next to William Ibotson.

VAGRANTS

The Ibbotson family tradition can be questioned but stories that are equally fascinating are frequent in the records of the Quarter Sessions. When Leonard Weatherhead was apprehended in the West Riding in

November 1745 he was examined by a magistrate and had a strange and exciting tale to tell. Until he was twelve years old he had lived in Ingleton, the place of his birth, and then for the next four years was hired out to farmers in Westmorland and north Lancashire. He earned 50s a year with Joseph Craven of Kendal and £3 a year with John Bushby of Sawrey. A major change in his life came when he was hired as a seaman by a merchant called Mr Robert Gilpin and placed on board the *Confirmation* bound from Whitehaven to Antigua. In his new position he was paid 30s a month and no doubt thought he was improving his lot.

However, under circumstances which his petition does not make clear, he and the rest of the crew abandoned the ship after only three months, and the young seaman, who was still in his teens, made his way back to Whitehaven via Liverpool, first by packet boat and then by sloop. He took a job there as an ostler but after two years was out of work, although he did not say why. There followed a period of five years or so, during which time he did such farm work as came his way, but he then returned to sea under Captain Robert Thompson on a ship bound for Virginia, still in his early twenties. Unfortunately, two Spanish privateers captured the vessel and the English prisoners were taken to St Sebastian. They were there only three months when an exchange of prisoners took place and they were returned to Spithead.

Leonard Weatherhead then had to make his way back to the north of England and was obliged to pay his own passage by sloop to Liverpool: he arrived in early November but probably had few resources and took to the roads as a beggar. Having been arrested in Quarmby, a locality near Huddersfield, he was questioned by Justice Radcliffe and told him of his plight. There seems to have been little sympathy and as he had no obvious legal settlement he clearly posed a problem. That was made worse because he was accompanied by a woman called Ann who was his wife or so he claimed. The magistrate handed the young couple over to the constable who was ordered to convey them to Littleborough in Lancashire, as the first stage of a journey to Sawrey. He was still only twenty-seven but it was over ten years since he had worked there as a hired man. Nevertheless, Sawrey was deemed to be the place of his last legal settlement.

The explanations and excuses of vagrants, exaggerated or not, paint an unforgettable picture of travellers on the highways. A group apprehended at Steeton in 1742 were suspected of being pickpockets, and the judgement passed on them was damning: they were 'drunken, idle wanderers' sleeping in barns and unable to 'give a good account of themselves, some of them pretending to be seafaring persons, others to tell fortunes, and using subtil crafts to deceive his Majesty's subjects'; Robert Westhall had pretended 'to have skill in physick and surgery, without licence'; Henry Johnson had 'got his livelihood by ... using juggling and dexterity of hand, and eating fire'. Ilkley was the last place where he had performed his 'jugling tricks' and he had managed to pass through the town without being arrested; John Huthersay and his wife 'wandred to Skipton and were ... singing ballads there' when arrested.

The story of a vagrant taken by the constable in Gargrave in 1749 was picaresque in nature. Willam 'Crothorm' had been born in Ireland but moved across to Scotland about 1730 and lived there for a year before travelling south to Swaledale. Three years later, perhaps seeking stability, he settled in the Ripon area and married a widowed lady called Martha Richardson. They occupied a house in Ingerthorpe

Shown here is a recruiting party from the 33rd Regiment, later the Duke of Wellington's Regiment. The acceptance of money, the 'prest', was legal proof of a man's engagement. An etching from George Walker's *Costume of Yorkshire* (1814). (*Author's collection*)

valued at £16 per annum and lived there about thirteen years. However, William 'was pressed for a souldier on account of an assault' and after his discharge at York moved south to Surrey looking for work. He returned to Yorkshire with a woman called Ann and married her in 1746, living in Markington. In the four or five years that followed he had farmed in Cumberland, in the parish of 'Crisp' (Kershope?) but was now again homeless and without any 'visible way of living'.

There is evidence that one or two vagrants were educated men who had fallen on bad times. In 1741, William Dowson, born in North-allerton, had travelled from place to place seeking business and selling 'Plasters and Powders for the worms'. He had no licence and no legal settlement but had been 'hired for a year to teach a schole in Midleton in Teasdale'. In the same year Henry Fawcett, whose wife sang ballads, was arrested as 'a common fidler'. He had formerly rented a farm in Richmond where he served the office of constable and paid taxes.

Many of those on the road, sleeping in barns by their own admission, were young women. Jane Wooler, arrested in Embsay in 1741 for begging, was a runaway apprentice, escaping 'severe treatment from her master's daughter', Alice Smith. Margaret Varley 'born as she hath always been told in the township of Martons both' had been a hired servant in Gargrave but chose to leave after six months to marry a labourer who then enlisted in the army. Things were even worse for Elizabeth Milner of Barden near Richmond. When she was brought before the magistrates for felony, in 1756, she told them she had married 'a Scotchman' called Ogilby in 1744 and had seven children by him before she discovered that he was a bigamist. Ogilby moved to London with his first wife abandoning Elizabeth and three surviving children. It was ordered that Elizabeth 'be whipped in Otley market' and then sentenced to hard labour in the House of Correction. A surviving letter from Mr William Lamplugh reveals that he thought she should be transported to the colonies.

EMIGRATION

The origins of those who were transported can be extremely difficult to trace. Nevertheless, Gwyneth Dow from Australia, whose maiden name was Terry, felt challenged by the remarkable story of Samuel Terry, a man who was convicted of felony in 1799 and transported to Australia the following year. Her account of this convict, who became the richest man in New South Wales and was dubbed 'the Botany Bay Rothschild', is a wonderful tale in its own right but equally fascinating is her account of the search itself. Much of her work was carried out in the North Riding and her comments on the Wensleydale landscape, the people she met in the dale and the stories she was told, turn a genealogical exercise into an absorbing piece of social and family history. She was successful finally in establishing a relationship between Samuel Terry and a certain John Terry who had grown up in Redmire before leaving for Tasmania.

Ironically, family historians in Yorkshire can often profit from research carried out here and overseas by descendants of those who left England, willingly or unwillingly. There are hundreds of published stories of emigrants which family historians in this country would find both interesting and useful. One such story links North America and Ribblesdale.

There is little evidence that families from the Dales made a significant contribution to what has been called the Great Migration, the

Slaidburn village. Peaceful enough now, but at the heart of Quaker persecution in the period up to 1682. In that year the Settle removal certificate authorised the departure from England of about thirty local people from seven different families. (*The author*)

settlement of New England, although one or two possible migrants have been named. However, when William Penn sailed for America in 1682, on board a ship called the *Welcome*, he was accompanied by many Yorkshire families, some of them certainly from the Dales. His was not the only ship to make the crossing and soon after his safe arrival he wrote of twenty-three others in the fleet, all with Quakers aboard. American scholars have researched the history of this fleet, attempting to name all the ships and compile passenger lists, so we know a good deal about the passengers, especially a group of six or seven Ribblesdale families who settled in what became Pennsylvania. Much of this information is contained in a copy of a document called the Settle Certificate that authorised their 'removal'. It was issued by the Settle monthly meeting and contained the distinctive local sur-names Cowgill, Croasdale, Hayhurst, Stackhouse, Walmsley, Walne and Wigglesworth, many of which can be traced to Ribblesdale. The circumstances in which that migration took place are well documented.

The Quakers or Society of Friends was established by George Fox in 1648–50 and it made many converts in the Yorkshire Dales where separatist societies had already been established. The sect may have preached tolerance and peace but their desire for reform brought them into direct conflict with members of the Church of England and it was not long before families and communities were split. As early as 1654 Cuthbert Hayhurst and Thomas Wigglesworth were taken into custody for 'breaking the peace upon the Lord's day' in Slaidburn church, accused of disturbing the congregation during the sermon. We can infer that they were outspoken in their criticisms, and they further angered their neighbours by refusing to find sureties for their good behaviour.

The first direct evidence we have that the Slaidburn Friends were meeting illegally is in a document of 1670. In November that year about a score of them were arrested, all adults, accused of coming together to 'preach and teach ... contrary to the liturgy and practice of the Church of England'. Several of the surnames that were later to feature in the Settle certificate were already prominent, that is: Croasdale, Hayhurst, Walne and Wigglesworth. Other local families involved were the Birketts and Walbanks. According to the informants the meeting had taken place 'within the house of Thomas Wigles-worth' but the farm was not named.

The barn at Skelshaw, reputedly where watch was kept when illegal meetings were held in Thomas Wigglesworth's house. (*The author*)

When further arrests were made in May 1671 the meeting-place was identified. Again a number of men and women were convicted of 'being at a conventickle or an unlawful meeteinge and assemblie' and on this occasion it was said to have taken place 'at the house of Thomas Wiglesworth of Skelshay'. Skelshaw is a farm in the township of Easington, high up on the edge of the moor, in an ideal location for secret gatherings. One or two of those arrested were exonerated by the court but Cuthbert Hayhurst was a persistent offender, so he was bound over and had his goods 'distrained'. Mary Wawne and Richard Croasdell of Waddington were also among the accused. The fact that the witness who alerted the authorities was Thomas Croasdale points to a division within that family.

Some of the depositions in these cases hint at the feelings aroused when families were split by their beliefs. For example, Edward Croasdale and Francis Frankland, the constable for Slaidburn, were responsible for taking Robert Walmsley back to Waddington after his arrest. Richard Croasdale was the constable there but when he was asked to deal with the prisoner and shown the warrant he refused to act on it and pushed it back into Frankland's pocket. Then, according to the Slaidburn men, he 'went his way laughinge, and in a derideinge manner sleighted the warrant and told them he would not obey them'. Not surprisingly this brought an angry response from the Justices who treated his actions as a case of contempt.

There were many other groups of Friends in the Dales who fell foul of the authorities in this difficult period. The formal wording of the indictment of a Beamsley meeting, in May 1665, exaggerated though it may be, reflects the fear and sense of outrage that the rest of the community felt. The accused were said to be 'endangering ... the publicke peace, to the terror of his Majesty's leige people' and many of them were fined. As in other cases the fines were exacted via a distraint of the offenders' goods which were then sold, a system that was manifestly open to abuse. The alternative was imprisonment in the common gaol and three months' hard labour, a dreadful experience for otherwise law-abiding people. Some of the family names here were Barber, Dodgson, Moon, Myers and, interestingly, Walmsley. At Little Stainforth, in June 1671, four people were arrested, but the principal sufferer was Samuel Watson who was fined £40 'for taking upon him to teach in his own house' and a further £20 for 'suffering the conventicle to be there'. He had long been a zealous and outspoken reformer, and that appears to have brought out the worst in some of those he tried to influence. In 1659 he interrupted the service in Giggleswick church and the people 'brok his head upon the seats'. The following year he was driven out of Burton in Bishopdale by a fellow 'with a great staff and pistol' who threatened to shoot him.

Another spate of indictments started in 1683, when the authorities took action against those who met unlawfully in William Holgate's house at Sawley. Richard Hoyle was the informant, and he claimed to have seen ten persons or more in Holgate's house. Among them were Thomas Driver of Gisburn, two men from Lancashire called Aspinall and Cowburn, and William Oddy of Martin Top in Rimington. Elsewhere in this western section of the dales there were arrests at Fewston, Askwith and Dent and it is the last of these that gives us some idea of the financial side of the arrests. The date was 13 January 1685 and the unlawful conventicle had been at the house of William Mason of Stonehouse. Just over £6 was raised by selling his goods, towards a fine of £20: John Mason had to pay over £9 and 'nine other hearers' 5s each. Also taken account of were the expenses of the

Knight Stainforth Hall, 1993. The prominent local Quaker Samuel Watson lived here and offered hospitality to itinerant ministers. The hall was licensed as a meeting-house for Quakers after the Act of Toleration in 1689. *(The author)*

constable and churchwardens, for their 'levying and disposinge of the goods' and 'His Majesty's third part' paid to the sheriff, Mr Tankard.

The persecution of the Quakers was often directly responsible for a family's departure to America. Bartholomew Longstreth, also on a certificate from Settle, is said to have left Yorkshire in 1699 and can be credited with having ensured the survival of his surname. Although several of the variants were listed in England in 1881 they were all very uncommon, whereas in America Longstreth is now well established. Much of the information that we have about these groups of Quakers is in the records of the Quarter Sessions but in the case of emigrants there is often a wide range of research material in America, ranging from primary sources to family histories of varying quality. It is interesting for example to open a printed copy of land records for Bucks County, Pennsylvania and see a transaction of 1706 that involved Thomas Stackhouse and was witnessed by Bartholomew Longstreth. Stackhouse too is far more numerous in America than it is in England.

Burlington, New Jersey, where many Yorkshire Quakers settled from the 1670s. The town takes its name from an old spelling of Bridlington. The author and his wife Ann-marie were made welcome there in 2008. (*Author's collection*)

NOVA SCOTIA

Between 1772 and 1775 more than 1,000 people left Yorkshire for Novia Scotia from ports on the east coast. Little is known here about the movement of so many families from the county and yet the emigrants played an important role in Canadian history on the cusp of the Revolutionary war. My own interest in the topic was awakened by a special 24–page supplement to the *Sackville Tribune Post* entitled 'Yorkshire 2000', part of a millennium project that culminated in a Conference at Mount Allison University. The conference title was 'Immigration and Impact: The Yorkshire Settlers from 1772 to the Present' and some sixteen lectures were devoted to aspects of the subject, including the influence that the immigrants had on vernacular architecture, the establishment of Methodism and their role in the Cumberland Rebellion.

These were farming families from north and east Yorkshire, not from the towns and villages of the West Riding, and many of their surnames hint at connections with the Dales: e.g. Fawcett, Jaques,

Metcalf, Sedgwick, Remmington, Routh, Stockdale and Tatham, but their exact origins are often far from clear. A group that has been traced to Coverdale consisted of Joshua and James Gildart or Geldart who travelled with Robert Leeming and a widow called Eleanor Harrison, aged forty-eight. They sailed from Hull in March 1774, on a ship named the *Albion*, in the company of 182 other emigrants 'all from Yorkshire'. We are fortunate to have details of their occupations, their ages and the reasons they gave for leaving England. Joshua aged forty-eight and his nephew John aged nineteen were 'husbandmen' or farmers, and they were hoping to purchase their own land in Nova Scotia: 'the great advance in rents' had influenced their decision. What is not generally known is that agents were based in Yorkshire in order to persuade dissatisfied farmers to leave for Nova Scotia. They were encouraged to emigrate by advertisements, pamphlets and promotional tracts; it was mass migration on a different scale from anything that had happened previously in Yorkshire. Something similar took place in Swaledale when lead mining declined. In *Yorkshire Tour* the authors said that in the depression of the early nineteenth century an

Advocate Bay, Nova Scotia. A typical landscape in the area where Yorkshire families settled in the 1770s. (*Author's collection*)

Coverham churchyard, 2005. John Geldart was nineteen years old in 1774 when he left Carlton for Nova Scotia. There were several Metcalfes among the emigrants, in 1772 and 1774. (*The author*)

office was opened in Hawes to arrange the passage of families to America. The final closing of the mines coincided with expanding growth in the textile industry, and cotton manufacturers are said to have sent horses and carts into the dale so that families and their furniture could travel free of charge to the Lancashire towns.

It is of interest to family historians to note the successful ramification of many of the families that left Yorkshire, especially those who moved overseas. When I was in Nova Scotia I checked the local telephone directories and found hundreds of entries for the surname Geldart. In Moncton alone the total was 110. Descendants of John Geldart have actively researched their family history and put their findings on line. The *Geldart Family Genealogy Forum*, for example, provides details which show that the migrant John married Martha Smith and they had ten children, including five sons. Their eldest son, also called John, had thirteen children, seven of whom were boys: twelve of the children married. Ironically the surname appears to have fared less well in the West Riding where the count in 1881 was just 108.

Chapter 7

The Quarter Sessions and Dales Life

The responsibilities of the Justices of Peace touched on many aspects of life in the local community, not just on law and order, and we have access to that information in the Quarter Sessions records, particularly the rolls. These documents regularly deal with the lower echelons of society and in them we discover more about the poor, who normally pose problems for family historians. The supporting depositions and petitions are invaluable for the insights they offer us, almost incidentally, into the daily activities of our ancestors and, because they are written in English and not Latin, we feel more in touch with those involved.

THE POOR

It was poor law legislation in the sixteenth century, particularly in Elizabeth's reign, that effectively made the state and not the church responsible for the relief of the poor in English society: after the monasteries were dissolved, new legislation established the principle that each parish had to make provision for its own impotent poor. A succession of Acts brought about major changes, and charitable relief gave way to relief via taxation of the better-off. Overseers of the poor were created and a local rating system established: these moves were followed by an Act in 1601 that was to be the foundation of poor law administration for well over 200 years.

Parish registers contain numerous examples of illegitimacy. In Giggleswick, for example, an unmarried girl called Isabel Banke gave birth in 1569 to a daughter Jenet; the father was Richard Lynsay, possibly of Lawkland. The following year Jenet Jackson, also a single woman, gave birth to a son and claimed that George Paslawe was the father. There can be information about such bastardy cases in the accounts of the overseers of the poor, if they survive, but if the matter was brought to the attention of the JPs we can hope to find the evidence in the Quarter Sessions records.

The new Acts made the parish responsible for the maintenance of an unacknowledged bastard child, with potential consequences for the rate payers. It became important to establish where a birth had taken place, who the father was, and which parish ought to pay. Additional Acts meant that 'lewd' women with chargeable bastards could be sent to the House of Correction, a law which some historians claim encouraged abandonment, abortion and infanticide: still births had to be witnessed. The impact of these strict new laws on the community is revealed in the documents.

A typical case occurs in a court order issued in Kildwick in June 1704. It had to do with 'a female bastard child, christened by the name of Joan, late born upon the body of Mary Leach in the townshipp of Embsey cum Eastby'. Mary Leach was a widow and the legal process had established that a local farmer called John Shackleton was the father, so arrangements were made 'for the reliefe and maintenance of

Beamsley Hospital, 1993. These were almshouses for the needy, built in 1593 by the Countess of Cumberland. The circular building is unusual in having a central chapel with several tiny rooms radiating from it. The chimneystacks are evidence of the four fireplaces in the diagonal sections. (*The author*)

the ... child and for the discharging and indempnifying the inhabitants'. These decisions were set out formally in a document and the major points are extracted below:

> Imprimis: Upon examinacion of ... Mary Leach and severall other persons upon oath ... we do find the said John Shackleton to be the only father ... the reputed father ... and further order ...
>
> Secondly that John Shackleton shall ... pay unto the churchwardens and overseers of the poor of Embsey cum Eastby ... the sum of two shillings per month and every month towards the releife and education of the ... child untill she shall attain the age of seaven years, being thought sufficient in regard of his poverty and mean estate, and it appeard she is a very lewd idle woman and he shall upon sight pay the sum of five shillings for charges expended dureing the month she lay in.
>
> Thirdly we do order that the child shall be kept and nourished by her mother untill she shall attain the age of seaven years ... so far as she is able ... with the said allowance ... which if she refuse to doe then John Shackleton shall take her from her mother and either bring her up or take care to see her brought up and shall likewise punish the mother as the law in such case directs.
>
> Fourthly and lastly we do order that when the child attain to 7 years the said John Shackleton shall either put her ... to be an apprentice ... and shall give security to the churchwardens and overseers of the poor of Embsey to keep harmless and indemnifyed the inhabitants ... from all manner of charges.

In similar circumstances Elizabeth Hurtley of Stainforth had a son Thomas baptised in 1684: the father was identified as Thomas Wharfe of Sannet Hall on the evidence of the midwife and a neighbour. They were named as Emma Tunstall of Horton in Ribblesdale and Agnes Whitfield of Westside House on Malham Moor. Thomas Wharfe presented a petition to the magistrates when the court met at Wetherby in which he conceded that he had fathered the child and expressed his willingness to 'give security to save the parish harmless'. Of course 'harmless' here means free from expense. Orders similar to those in the previous case were issued, and Thomas Wharfe was made responsible for maintaining the child and then putting it out apprentice.

There is clear evidence that some mothers, supported and encouraged by their neighbours and relatives, were not above naming as the 'father' a man of more substantial means than the actual father. In 1720, Elizabeth Garnet of Paythorne, described as 'a notorious, lewd woman' who already had two bastard children, had been 'taken in the act of fornication' and arrested. She threatened those who questioned her, saying that 'the next bastard born upon her body she would father upon Robert Dodgson', a well-to-do local resident. In 1706, at a family get-together in Keighley, Ann Leach was persuaded 'to father her bastard on Denis Stell and not Henry Hatch'. The depositions mention how this was achieved by bribes and drink but Ann repented 'before she gott to bed' and went back on what she had said, calling out 'God forgive me, I have fathered the child wrongfully'. This caused immediate alarm and Ann Hide replied 'Hold thy tongue, not a word of that or we are undone'.

In Bolton by Bowland, in 1731, it was 'the belief of all the neighbourhood' that George Broxapp was the father of Isabel Parker's bastard child, and yet 'by his persuasions' she had sworn before the magistrates 'that another person, very unluckily' was the father. During the trial it emerged that when Isabel Parker was in labour, the overseers of the poor had asked a midwife called Margaret Giffard to attend on her, and that Broxapp had burst violently into the house whilst she was helping the woman. He threatened her first of all, shouting that he would 'take care' of her if she did not deliver the baby quickly, and then said 'I suppose you will take her life if she does not father it upon me'.

In Dent, in 1672, the inhabitants sought to blacken the characters of a man called Edmond Waller and 'his pretended wife' Isabel, making out also that Edmond had no settlement in their parish. The twenty-six witnesses included Christopher Tennant, Leonard Willan, Alexander Thistlethwayte, Thomas Coupstacke and many other prominent local men. They claimed that Waller had arrived in the village thirty years earlier, from Barbon in Westmorland, and married a woman called Cragg who 'had a litle cottage house'. He had, they alleged, 'by his druncken and lude carriage [behaviour] soone sould and spent the sayd house', upon which he resorted to beating and abusing his wife, to such an extent that she became both blind and lame. They did not explain why they had stood by while this was happening but claimed to have provided him with 12d maintenance a week for many years. During that time Waller had fathered several bastard children, one to a woman called Staveley and two to a woman called Bower. His drunkenness had continued but when his wife died he fled to Dublin with Isabel Fearne, a woman with whom he had been 'keepinge dayly company'. He was away three years and then returned, threatening to 'make the parish mayntayne both him and her'. The Dent townsmen thought that he should be removed 'to the place of his last settlement' – presumably Barbon – so as to free the parish of 'such a wicked, debayst fellow'.

Many girls were prepared to give detailed accounts of how they were made pregnant. In 1718, Martha Brooksbank of Keighley claimed that she was 'begott with a bastard child at one John Beanland's – upon the floor, in the house boddy, she being a servant there'; in 1726, also in Keighley, two other servants had made love 'in a chamber over the shopp, upon a parcel of wool'. Martha Wood had become pregnant in 1710 after two meetings with John Hill, the first time 'at night ... after Bingley Tyde', the local fair, and the second 'in a cow boose in the mistall'. I believe the girls were trying to avoid being described as 'lewd', the word used for habitual offenders who were dealt with more severely. Perhaps they offered the details in the hope that the magistrates would view what had taken place as an isolated instance, quite out of character. Usually they managed to imply that they were almost innocent parties in what had taken place and they certainly wanted the magistrates to believe in their naivety and essentially good character. In 1685, Alice Taylor of Horton in Ribblesdale claimed that she had been seduced 'through many pretences and faire promises'; Elizabeth Guy of Settle (1724) was misled 'through wheedlings and promises' – promises of marriage, no doubt.

At other times we are made aware of the desperate situations in which girls found themselves. Alice Whittaker of Skipton claimed that 'her own father did beget her with child' (1735) and the records show that he made no attempt to deny it. In 1690, Ellen Watson had an amazing story to tell about her unmarried sister, Mary Goodgion of Snaygill. She had suspected that Mary was pregnant but had to leave the house with her husband to help a neighbour with his heifer. On her return she 'found Mary in bed, newly delivered of a bastard female child' which now lay beside her. What followed is best told in Ellen's own words:

> She and John Gill of Bradley, the father, thereupon towards night
> time did swaddle and lapp up the child with wool and warme

cloaths ... and they agreed that Henry Watson should convey [it] carefully in the night to some place where itt might soon be found befor itt tooke harme, in order to prevent the shame of her sister's having a bastard.

When Henry returned in the morning he told how he had carefully left the child 'upon a bench att a house in Burley Woodhead', at which point the story was taken up by Ann Whitehead who said:

that her father Lawrence Whitehead, being the first of the family out of dooers that morning, about 4 of the clock, found a female child about a day or two old laid upon a bench near his out doer, well and warmly lappt up with wooll about the feete, hipps and necke, left on purpose for the towne to take care on and to keep the parties that owned it from discoverie.

A similar story was told by Katherine Sturth of Rathmell who was delivered of a male child at Long Preston in 1695. Shortly afterwards she walked with her baby to Knapton, near York, a journey of at least forty-five miles, and there she left it in 'a winter corne field, nigh the highway and then withdrew herselfe some distance'. After watching for some time she saw a man 'come that way who took it upp and carryed it away'. The father in this case was an excise man from Hunslet who had met Katherine by chance at harvest time.

A distressing testimony is that of Mary Atkinson of Waddington, in 1709, who may have been the employer of Mary Midgley, the unmarried girl at the centre of the affair. She says how she 'went to Cliderow, there being a fair there ... and left Mary Midgley sicke in bed in her house, but did not thinke she had been with child'. When she returned home she was met by Ann Giles who had been asked to look after the sick girl and Ann 'shewed her something on a pewter dish which she told her was a child'. After some time, she said, 'the child was run all to water' and Mary Atkinson 'threw it out of doors, about 5 a clocke the same night'. Mary Midgley told her that 'a lad in Yorkshire had begotten it'.

Under the new Poor Law Acts, with each township or parish responsible for its own poor, the terms 'settlement' and 'removal' acquired new shades of meaning. When an individual fell on hard times it was his legal settlement that entitled him to relief via the poor rate, and that right was determined in a number of ways, especially by

Spence's Hospital, Carleton in Craven. It was built for ten poor widows by Ferrand Spence at the very end of the seventeenth century. In the attractive courtyard is a wooden gallery on stone pillars and the front entrance has a tall, iron gate with impressive gate-piers. (*The author*)

birth or residence. Of course, individuals and families continued to move around, whether shiftlessly or in pursuit of a better life, and these migrations inevitably complicated the issue. A poor person who could not prove his settlement was therefore likely to be 'removed', that is sent back to where he had come from. It was an issue that gave rise to countless disputes as township officials looked for ways of saving money.

One result was that parish officers kept their eyes on poor women who were pregnant and unmarried. The aim was to have the offending individual or family removed and the financial burden shifted to another township. Inevitably, such incidents could be very divisive: in 1673, the inhabitants of Hawkswick sent a petition to the magistrates asking that John Verity be removed to Litton, the neighbouring township. Litton was actually in the same parish as Hawkswick but each place was responsible for its own poor so neighbourly feelings were put aside. The reason given was that John Verity's wife was 'greate with child'. Occasionally, a family was split by such a removal order: in 1731, when Jane Thomas and two of her three children were removed from Langcliffe to Burnley, the order did not apply to her bastard son Thomas who 'not being born in Burnley ought not to be sent thither'.

The information in these cases can link families in different villages and provide items of genealogical interest. In 1750, when Christopher Watson of Cononley was 'old and impotent', the court placed responsibility for him on Hugh Watson, his son, and William Cryer of Carleton, his son-in-law. We learn also how the authorities reacted if the closest relatives were themselves impoverished. In the 1660s, Frances Ripley's husband died and she married a Thirsk tanner called Thomas Jackson. Sadly, she died soon afterwards leaving three young children, all under ten. Jackson claimed that he was unable to support the children as he had 'neither reall nor personal estate' so the search turned elsewhere. Two possible relatives were named, the first being Dorothy Mann of Bramley near Grewelthorpe, Frances's mother: she was the widow of William Mann the elder 'gentleman' and that was enough for the court to order her to take one of the children. The second relative was John Ripley of Kirkby Malzeard, the children's grandfather. He had already accepted one of the children but was now ordered to care for the third.

Settlement could also be determined by apprenticeship or working contracts. In 1739, for example, an out-of-work William Shackleton was living with his family in Idle, near Calverley, and the magistrates ordered his removal to Keighley. The reason given was that he had served his apprenticeship with Thomas Brigg of Keighley before getting married and moving to Calverley. That determined his settlement and he was therefore removed to Keighley with his wife Hannah and five children: they were named as William, Hannah, Jeremy, Martha and Ellen.

A dispute between the townships of Arncliffe and Long Preston illustrates the importance that could be placed on a hiring agreement. Andrew Whitfield of Long Preston, said to be 'a Scotchman', was no longer able to look after himself by 1722. In an effort to have him removed from the parish the Long Preston officers provided evidence of his employment back in the 1680s, when he had been hired to serve John Hammond of Arncliffe. He had worked there for a time, earning £3 10s per annum, but moved to Long Preston three years later and 'bought a little cottage' there. Because of his earlier contract to John Hammond he was sent back to Arncliffe!

Barden Tower, over a century ago. In 1726, George Thompson was on his way there at 1 o'clock in the morning, when he chanced upon a gang of men fishing illegally in the Wharfe with 'shackle netts' (QS1/65/5). (*Author's collection*)

In other cases the depositions provide evidence of the distances that some individuals travelled. A maintenance case in Skipton, in 1690, concerned Mary Heath who had married Richard Croft some nine years earlier in London. He had now 'runne away from her' and was refusing to support their two children. Her father-in-law, Richard Croft the elder, accepted responsibility for her son George but refused to do anything for her daughter Lydia. Even more distressing was the testimony of Sarah Jackson alias Wright, a woman from Wisbech who had been picked up as a vagrant in Bingley. She told the magistrates that her deceased husband Stephen Wright had confessed on his death bed that he also had a wife and four children in Bingley. Her long journey north suggests that she had been hoping for financial assistance.

The case of Leonard Weatherhead was quoted earlier to show how mobile a vagrant could be. There are numerous similar biographies, and it is difficult to imagine how any other source could offer us such detailed personal histories. The fascinating appeal of Thomas Benson of Burnsall, arrested for peddling without a licence, was heard at Skipton on 11 July 1710:

> Sheweth – that your pet[itioner] servd an apprenticeshipp att Ripley and Patley Bridge to the trade of a mercer and grocer, And above twenty years together kept a grocer's shop in Patley Bridge. That your petitioner above fifteen years agoe removd to Burnsall, where he likewise excercisd the same trade, till by losses and misfortunes and a great charge of children, hath reducd your petitioner to poverty whoe notwithstanding his age of sixty yeares could much contribute towards the support and maintenance of himself, his wife and foure children, in case he could be allowd to travell five or six miles from his own habitacon, to sell tobacco and some small wares belonging to his trade, which hee designs to carry on his back, purely for the assistance of himself and family, if it please god to restore him to his former health, being now very badly. And not able to buy or carry any goods to the vallue of 20s his substance being soe small.

Thomas Benson then asked the magistrates to give his petition serious consideration and grant an order that would allow him to travel into the neighbouring towns to sell the commodities he had suggested. At the bottom of the document is the single word 'rejected'.

FIRE AND FLOOD

The value of a fire to our ancestors cannot be overestimated, for it was both a source of warmth and comfort and a means of cooking food. A fire under control was an enormous asset whereas a fire out of control could bring disaster to individuals and communities. With no cover from insurance companies and no body organised to fight accidental fires, they were a very real threat to both lives and livelihoods. From the eighteenth century, local newspapers began to include reports of fires and the reports make it clear how great a problem they were: for the earlier period we are again dependent on the Quarter Sessions for information.

An early incident at Kilnsey in Wharfedale had to do with a family called Batty. On 13 July 1675, Richard Batty sought help from the authorities after 'a sudden accident of fire' burnt down his dwelling house and barn, together with all his hay. He had also, he said, lost 'much of his household stuffe and other goods' and was 'quite beggered'. The inference is that the fire had happened several months earlier but that Richard had initially found some sort of lodging. However, since then he had been 'twice turned out of doores' and was unable to find anywhere permanent to live.

Part of the problem seems to have been Anne Batty, Richard's wife, a woman with the reputation of a trouble-maker. At the same July court an order was issued for her arrest, and the statement leading up to that describes her as 'a person of bold carriage, frequentlie useinge her tongue scouldingelie ... and detractingelie of the neighbourhood'. She was a notorious gossip 'carryinge tales and false reports between neighbour and neighbour, towne and towne, howse and howse'. Even so, the inhabitants of Kilnsey were ordered to seek the assent of their manorial lord and 'erect a cottage house' for Richard Batty on the waste. Although they were also ordered to pay him 2s 6d weekly, documents from the October meeting of the court indicate that neither of these orders had been acted on. They were renewed by the local JP Cuthbert Wade and, as no further petitions have been located, we can perhaps presume that the cottage was built.

Another trouble-maker was Joseph Clough of Broughton, near Skipton, a butcher by trade but an arsonist when in his cups. In 1690, the magistrates were obliged to listen to a catalogue of this man's misdemeanours that started with stone-throwing at night time and included wilful damage, theft and assault. The victim of his assault on this occasion was John Ellis who said that Clough kept bad company and frequently got drunk – he 'did not mind his worke to live by it like others' but lived 'an idle, scandalous life'. John Lofthouse told how Clough 'did once bring fire and sett it in the straw under his own house easing' with the intention of setting the whole town on fire. At a time when many buildings were still thatched that was a very real threat.

It is noticeable that John Lofthouse spoke in his deposition of Clough 'bringing' fire and setting it in the straw, a reminder that safety matches were not then available. A case heard in 1711 was about a house fire at Harrogate which Henry Spink judged to have started 'in the thatch on the inside, att the foote of a spar'. He had found what he called a fire-stick in that location, and the same object was mentioned by Anne Walker, another witness. According to her she had been visited by a woman called Katherine Hardcastle who had come into the house 'to gett a fire, pretending to kindle a fire in her owne house'. She had taken the fire-stick back with her and Anne Walker believed that she had used it to set fire to the house she lived in.

Among the most interesting documents in cases of fire are the inventories of goods. George Haigh was a flax-dresser whose house in Knaresborough was destroyed by fire in 1715. The cost of repairing it was put at just over £78, based on accounts submitted by masons and carpenters, whereas the value of the stock he had lost, in the house, cellar and shop, amounted to almost twice that sum. It consisted mostly of huge quantities of hemp, flax and 'tow', much of it un-processed, but there were also '32 dosen of drest hemp and line', some line yarn and 'candle weak'. We are familiar now with candlewick as the name of a soft cotton material but that meaning dates only from the 1930s. George Haigh's 'candle weak' was doubtless tow or hemp made up, somewhat ironically, into wicks for candles.

Just two years earlier, in 1713, there was a disastrous fire at Healthwaite Hill near Harewood. It destroyed Timothy Waite's farm buildings, the crops they housed and a variety of husbandry materials – losses estimated at £128. One of the buildings destroyed was said to be a 'helme' – an interesting word, found in Yorkshire from the 1400s. It is often defined as a shed for cattle or crops but here it had a more important function for Timothy Waite kept a cart and a wain in it. In

1642, another Yorkshire farmer wrote of running 'the waines under the helmes'.

An inventory for Richard Burley of Spofforth, for goods 'lately consumed by fire', was drawn up in December 1730. Part of the interest here lies in the fact that we have both the original list, in a bold but not very well-educated hand, and the final draft for the authorities, immaculately written. We can therefore compare a spelling like 'doaf trofe', which preserves the dialect pronunciation, with 'dough trough'. Vernacular terms replaced by the scribe include 'crab juce' by 'verjuice'; 'seeing glass' by 'looking glass' and 'winder cloth' by 'winnowing cloth'. Changes at which we have to smile are 'accoutrements' in place of 'materials' and the transformation of the surname Burley into Burleigh. These were clearly intended to add a touch of class and make the final draft more persuasive.

The elements often played a part in such disasters. In a fire at Follifoot, in 1690, the losses were put at just over £516 and the record in the Quarter Sessions blames the hot June weather. It also captures something of the dreadful impact the event had on those who witnessed it:

> Upon Munday, the second day of June ... there hapned a most sad and laymentable fire within the towne of Follyfoote which was soe suden and unexpected that in the space of one houer [it] burnt downe fouer dwelling houses and fouer barns the season being soe extreame hott and drye att that instant time cawsed the fire to be more cruell and tearrable that most of there hous[ehold] stuffe where consumed.

At that time many houses still had thatched roofs and once a fire caught hold there was little that people could do. On 11 March 1723, at five o' clock in the afternoon, a 'sudden and dreadfull fire' started in Wetherby and in a very short time it had consumed dwelling houses, stables, barns, brew-houses, granaries, warehouses, shops and a smithy. Aided by 'the violence of a south wind which blew very high' it destroyed grain, wearing apparel and a wide range of shop and household goods. There are pages of detail recording the losses of over forty families and individuals, among them Mrs Mary Banks, for example, who had several buildings burnt down. The cost of replacing these was put at £774. The total for the town came to over £7,500. This fire is not always mentioned in accounts of Wetherby but it may help to explain why Arthur Mee described the town as 'a famous little place with nothing much to see'.

SHEEP STEALING

Numerous cases of sheep stealing were brought to the attention of the courts and that emphasises the importance that the animal had in the local economy. It may also reflect the influence of the magistrates, many of whom had a vested interest as landholders with vulnerable flocks. Whether or not that is true the many depositions provide us with snapshots of life in the Dales.

It may have been relatively easy to drive sheep away from their pastures but having to conceal the animals, dead or alive, was another matter, especially as the inedible parts bore the marks of individual owners. We have already seen how carcases or parts of a carcase were hidden in old mine workings – down 'grove' holes – but another favourite location was a dry-stone wall. In 1675, John Frankland of High Field, Slaidburn missed one of two sheep that had been 'coupled together having either of them a lambe' but a search of a house on Stephen Moor implicated George Harrison in the theft. They 'found the belly and the gutts ... greene and newly pauncht' in a ditch and then pieces of fresh mutton and lamb in a large poke 'in a wall fense within 20 rood or lesse of his fire house'.

Just a year earlier, Robert Scott of Threap Green, Bolton by Bowland, was seen 'to take several pieces of mutton out of a pott and putt them in his breeches, and goe up into a loft where he ... did putt them through a loupe hole into his neighbour's layth'. In 1670, the constable searched the house of George Fisher in Kirkby Malzeard and found a quarter of lamb, some blood in a bowl, seven fleeces in a chamber, much loose wool and four lambs' feet in a bushel: there were also 'one or two sheep panches new put in the midding' whilst a lamb skin was discovered 'in the briches of William Fisher'. At Ilkley, in 1729, a large quantity of 'melted sheeps sewet in 2 cakes' was discovered 'in the Bed straw in the parlor of John Gott'. Of course we learn nothing about the successful hiding-places.

In 1675, Mary Barrett was forced to confess that mutton found 'in a harden poke in a private place within the chimney corner within the ground' had been given to her by her son-in-law Henry Craven of Giggleswick. When Henry was examined he said that he and Richard Clarke of Rathmell had brought ten sheep down off Malham Moor, of

Mastiles Lane, the old route from Malham Moor to Kilnsey, sometimes called Bordley Mastiles. It derived its name from the Bordley pasture grounds and ran to the south and south-east of the High Mark. (*The author*)

which three were 'taken foorthe and killed and the rest driven upp againe'. On another occasion he had taken two sheep out of a barn belonging to William Newhouse the younger, killed one of them and then led the other on a rope 'to be secured in Lancliffe Springs'. Unfortunately for the thieves the animal made its escape 'with a rope at his hornes' and the trail led the constable to Henry Craven. Henry was a desperate fellow as his mother in law's evidence reveals:

> she hath severall times better advised and counselled and fore-warned him these practises, but hath beene putt in great danger and jeopardy of her life for so doeing and particularly one time the said Henry Craven and her other son in law Francis Younge had prepared poison for her to give in a cupp of drinke at Settle.

Mary Barrett was not the only woman to despair of the men in her family. When Peter Gifford of Rathmell was questioned about some sheep stolen from Thomas Armitsteade, in 1672, she was reported as saying: 'I would I were a hundred miles of – they are happy that hath a husband that will worke for his liveinge truely'. Her testimony provides us with more details of hiding places; a garden wall and 'a heape of stones before the house doore', with vivid images of the dispersed body parts of the slaughtered animals. These were found in the house and outbuildings that belonged to Peter Gifford but he protested that he knew 'nothing of them – exceptinge the skins and bones which were of some sheepe of his owne which dyed of themselves'.

There are several bits of local information in a Bordley case of 1673. The accused man on this occasion was Edward Verity who lived 'near the Barke Toppe': he claimed never to have stolen a sheep but found one by chance 'lying in a pasture called Bordley High Marke and did ... kill the said sheep there, taking the skinne of itt'. Once again the incriminating fleece was thrown into 'an old mine or grove hole' and the meat taken home and boiled. Richard Greenebanke who was 'the common herd for Bordley High Marke' found the skin and 'by the marke on itt' identified it as the property of Simon Wilkinson 'of Knowle bancke'. The reference to a common herdsman on the High Mark is confirmation that a number of farmers had stints on this vast upland pasture: Lee Gate High Mark and Bordley High mark are still shown on OS maps. As the same place-name is found also in Kildwick

Bordley, a Domesday vill. It became part of the Fountains Abbey estate and the Proctor family were named as tenants from the fifteenth century. (*The author*)

and Embsay it may be that High Mark once had generic significance regionally, possibly referring to the upper limit of the pastures concerned. 'Hye Mark' was used in connection with a Kilnsey pasture as early as 1538.

Almost inevitably the depositions tell us a good deal about the marks of different owners. In 1688, 'wether hogs' of Cuthbert Wade that had either strayed or been stolen from pastures in 'Oldcoates' had been 'markt with his own Ear and Tarr markes': the animals were found and identified at Bank Newton a dozen miles away. That mark had been defaced and 'other new markes set on, viz one stroake down the neer ribs, one other down the taylehead and a prop of the farr hook-bone all with Rud'. On the other hand, the sheep of James Place of Clapham had 'a burn in the horn mark'd J.P.' (1724) and John Tillotson of Lothersdale had a ewe taken that was 'clipp'd and mark'd with the mark of Henry King and burnt on the horn' (1726). In 1670, Robert Harper of Swinsty bought one ewe from his sister and 'the marke of itt was a piece of the Ear cutt of and a H on the near side'. It was found later in the possession of Joseph Waterworth of Clifton.

LEAD MINING

The mining of lead was an important local industry at the heart of many cases, and a petition sent to the magistrates at Skipton in July 1710, indicates that large sums of money were involved. The document was an appeal by Catherine Robinson, a widow, who claimed to be in a desperate situation and in need of financial support. Her appeal is worth quoting in full:

> ... about a month before Christmas last year your petitioner's husband dyed and left foure small children and your petitioner then bigg with child and left nothing but a few household goods to which your petitioner took administracon but before shee could obtaine the same, both shee and her children were likely to perish both for want of food and fireing, And afterwards your petitioner made a sale of most of her goods towards payment of her husbands debts and maintenance of her children, soe that your petitioner has nothing left to relieve her self and her family, save the milk of one cow, which belongs to the inhabitants of the said towneshipp. That your petitioners husband lived in good creditt and repute and caused above twoe thousand pounds to be spent

in the leadworks within the parish of Kettlewell And your petitioner had part of a grove or mine work in Starbotton but for want
of moneys and assistance, in the management thereof, the said
work is lost, soe that your petitioner has nothing left, either to
provide fire or victualls, but must inevitably perish without some
reliefe from the inhabitants of Buckden and Starbotten towards
the support of her self and five very small children.

Catherine Robinson then asked that her 'sad and deplorable condicon'
be taken into consideration and that she be granted 'such weekly
allowance' as they thought fair. A note in the margin states that when
the overseer of the poor of Starbotton learned of the intended petition,
he discharged a poor woman who had been assisting with Catherine's
children so that she would not be able to attend the sessions. The case
was referred.

A Buckden dispute some ten or eleven years later concerned the
alleged theft of some mining tools and a quantity of slag or waste.
Once again the rights and wrongs of the case are actually of less
interest than the incidental details that emerge in the depositions.
These make it clear, for example, that business agreements were
entered into by miners from over a relatively wide area and that loose
partnerships were formed in a very informal way, almost certainly in
the local alehouse. In this case the parties included a miner from
Swaledale, two from Buckden and Kettlewell and one from Glusburn,
three quite distinct lead-mining districts. Some of the miners' names
were very distinctive but did not have a local origin, e.g. Glenton,
Weare and Carrack, and it is interesting to speculate where the men
might have come from. On the other hand, several of the interested
parties who were not miners or smelters were almost certainly local
men. William Chapman of Starbotton was a carrier, engaged to transport 105 loads of cinders from Horton in Ribblesdale to Buckden, at a
rate of one shilling a load; John Slinger was the Buckden shoemaker,
appointed to 'cry a sale by the way of auxion and sell the wast of lead
ore and slaggs'. The sum of money thus realised seems quite high, for
Roger Harrison of Glusburn bid £18 for the waste which was to be
'worked over'. There are records from the fifteenth century of slag
being re-smelted.

The witnesses referred to several mines in Buckden, one of them
named Gavel and another at Buckden Gill Head, possibly quite small

C. CHAPMAN, MAIL CONTRACTOR,

GRASSINGTON, nr. SKIPTON,

Begs to inform the public that

THE ROYAL MAIL

Leaves Skipton Post Office at 6 a.m., and returns from Buckden at 3-40 p.m. On Sundays it leaves Skipton Post Office at 8-45 a.m., and returns from Buckden at 2 p.m.

A SECOND MAIL

Leaves Grassington at 5-45 a.m., Linton, 8-55 a.m., Cracoe, 9-15 a.m., Rylstone, 9-30 a.m., arriving at Skipton at 10-10 a.m. Returning from Skipton Post Office, 5 p.m., arriving at Rylstone at 6 p.m., Cracoe, 6-10 p.m., Linton, 6-35 p.m., Grassington, 6-45 p.m.

HE ALSO

RUNS A SECOND 'BUS

From Skipton to Buckden, from April to Oct.,

Leaving Skipton Station at 8-45 a.m., calling at Rylstone, Cracoe, Linton, Grassington, Coniston, Kilnsey, Kettlewell, and Starbotton, leaving Grassington per return at 6 p.m. On Sundays this 'Bus leaves Skipton Station at 7-30 a.m.

A DAILY 'BUS FROM GRASSINGTON TO SKIPTON.

Leaving Grassington at 7 a.m., and returning from Skipton Station at 3 p.m.

STABLES : THANET'S ARMS HOTEL, SKIPTON. POST HORSES AND CONVEYANCES AT REASONABLE CHARGES.

TEMPERANCE HOTEL: GOOD ACCOMMODATION FOR VISITORS AND TOURISTS.

The Chapman family were involved in transport up and down Wharfedale for generations. They were named as carriers in the Buckden lead-mining dispute in 1720 and this advertisement appeared 200 years later in Edmund Bogg's *Wharfedale*. It is in itself a small piece of family history. (*Author's collection*)

enterprises at the time. More surprising perhaps are the repeated references to 'all the smelt mills' in Buckden which might imply that each of the mines had its own mill. One of these was named in the evidence as Birks Mill and a second was described as an 'old ruinated mill', but the way the sentence is phrased suggests that there were others. There was also a 'chop kill' or kiln in the township.

A case in 1692 suggests that miners might be familiar enough with particular batches of ore to recognise where they came from. The alleged guilty party was John Alcock of Burnsall and his accusers were two miners called Francis Hullah and Thomas Grange, employees of Messrs Beckett and Tennant. They were employed 'in the working of a lead mine on a place called Elbolton' and reported that a quantity of lead was missing – 'betwixt six and seven dish'. Having secured a warrant they searched the houses of men under suspicion and in a chamber of John Alcock's house found a small quantity of ore, about 'three quarters of a dish'. They claimed to recognise it, saying that it was 'taken out of Elbolton which they can testify because they know some particular lumps ... which were of their own getting'. More ore was found in Alcock's field barn and once again the two miners recognised pieces from Elbolton. The word 'dish' signified a specific amount, as much as might be contained in a wooden trough or box, and the term is explained in a contemporary glossary, along with the dimensions of the dish. It was twenty-eight inches long, four deep and six wide.

There are many more documents in these papers which have to do with the theft of lead and lead ore. In 1688, for example, Thomas Coates of Darley explained that he had lead in his possession because 'att the smelt house he could, for two pence, have a laddle full of lead given to him'. William Fleetham explained that a piece of lead found in his possession had no mark upon it when he bought it and was now smaller, since he had 'cutt about a pound weight from it for making of hail – little bulletts to shutt [shoot] in a pistoll'. Such depositions may tell us very little but sometimes the words used by the parties involved are of interest, and we are also presented with cameos of life in the seventeenth century that it would otherwise be difficult to find.

Chapter 8
Bridges and Highways

The building and maintenance of bridges in Yorkshire is a subject that touches on many aspects of local history, and a wide range of documents is available, many of them again in the Quarter Sessions records. They include petitions, contracts, builders' accounts and numerous depositions from the Tudor and Stuart periods, all of which enlighten us about the regional vocabulary used by our ancestors and their bridge-building practices. Although less is available for earlier centuries, material has survived for the important bridges at Catterick and Kildwick. The contract for Catterick Bridge, dated 1422, has been published several times and is well known to local historians but information about Kildwick has only recently been published in full.

KILDWICK BRIDGE 1304–10

In *Bolton Priory* (1973) Ian Kershaw offered us a tantalising insight into the part played by the priory in the early history of Kildwick Bridge, first mentioned in thirteenth-century charters. Now, he and David Smith have completed a full transcription of the *Bolton Priory Compotus 1286–1325* (2000) and it means that we can analyse the entries for 1304–10 that relate to the building of a new stone bridge at Kildwick.

Bolton enjoyed a decade of relative prosperity from 1305 with favourable harvests, a growth in the sheep flock and an increase in revenue. It was a good time for investment and it made sense for the priory to create better access to those parts of the estate that were on the south side of the river Aire, principally the townships that lay within the parish of Kildwick. One or two contributions towards the expense of building the bridge were by local people. A lady called Julian de Craven made a gift of 6s 8d, and an unnamed donor gave the priory a cow which realised 7s 6d when it was sold. The total expenditure was said to be over £90 which was a considerable sum at that time but the bridge was being built of stone and most of that had to be taken to the site. Indeed, there are entries that relate to the

Kildwick Bridge. It has four arches, two rounded and two pointed, and they span
*c.*40 metres, a width that allows for flooding. The ribbed vaulting on the near side of
the arch dates from 1304–10 but the bridge was widened in 1780 and the plain
abutment is of that period. (*The author*)

carriage of stones by cart although some may also have been moved by
pack horses.

The men working on the bridge did not have hereditary surnames
so we find references in the accounts to John the carter (carectarius),
Ralph the quarrier and Thomas the mason (cementarius): Thomas
appears to have been the master mason who directed building work
on Skipton church in the years 1303–8. Although other masons are not
mentioned by name, we can note allowances made to them over and
above their wages. Their food was part of the expenditure and they
lived together as a group. It is not stated exactly where they ate and
slept but we can imagine that for several years a lodge near the bridge
would have been their temporary home.

Ralph 'le Quarreur' had been employed by the priory for some years
on different parts of the estate but in 1309 he was working at the

bridge, breaking stone. It reminds us that there were three distinct stages in the preparation of the building-stone, defined by the three medieval by-names Stonehewer, Stonebreaker and Stonewright. It is not possible to say what route John and Ralph would have taken to the bridge for we do not know the location of the quarry that provided the stone. Perhaps it was at Embsay, for the name Quarrier became hereditary and the family were taxed and paid rent in Embsay in 1379–1473. It would have been a difficult journey but presumably the carts followed a fairly direct route through Skipton, avoiding many of the hills. In contracts for other bridges, later than this, there was often provision made for a lime-kiln on the site, but here the first mention of a kiln was towards the end of the work. Perhaps they were discovering the best working practices as they progressed.

Much of their work has survived, and the present structure serves to remind us of the role played by the monasteries in creating and maintaining good communications. Margaret Slack thought the bridge 'must be one of the oldest in the north of England' whilst David Harrison noted that the investment of £90 'exceeded by a considerable margin the other investments made by the Priory … in those years'.

THE YORK TO KENDAL HIGHWAY

The Quarter Sessions material for bridges in the North Riding is earlier than that for the West Riding but the published volumes lack the detail found in the West Riding rolls. Nevertheless, they provide us with valuable information which can be profitably linked with items from other sources. Mentioned with great frequency are bridges 'on the direct road between the City of York and the vill of Kendall', a route through Wensleydale that was important even in the Middle Ages, linking great abbeys and castles with the wider world. In December 1588, Ulshaw Bridge was in need of repair and a letter has survived to the Justices of Peace which refers to 'the veiwinge of the decaie'. Having taken the advice of 'skilfull and expert workmen', the surveyors calculated that the bridge was in such a state of ruin that 200 marks would be 'little enough for the repairinge and paving thereof'. As an allowance was made for 'old timber' the inference is that it was still a wooden bridge. The expenditure was approved in January so it is surprising to discover that the authorities were still discussing the 200 marks in 1591. In 1593 a further sum was required

Middleham Castle, a royal fortress in the fifteenth century and testimony to the power of the Nevilles. The twelfth-century keep rises above the later curtain wall. The road near by that runs through the dale was formerly part of the major route between York and Kendal. (*The author*)

for the repair of part of the bridge, 'latelie fallen, and of some other part of it being in peril to fall'. It is difficult to know whether this referred to the original 'decay' or more recent damage to a newly-repaired bridge. The records certainly create the impression that progress was very slow and this raises questions as to how travellers fared in the meantime. Occasional references to temporary ferries suggest that repairs could take place over a long period.

Perhaps the JPs were overwhelmed by the recurrent need to raise money across the whole Riding for they were responsible for a large number of County Bridges and those in Wensleydale were a constant drain on their resources. In 1602, a sum of £120 was required for 'Aiskarth' Bridge, and Kilgram Bridge at Jervaulx was in need of repair the same year: in 1606 it was Masham Bridge that was in great ruin and decay, as was Yore Bridge 'a little from Bainbrigg' in 1607. Kilgram was again brought to their attention in 1611 and the phrase 'in need of present repair' seems to emphasise the need for urgent action. The magistrates expressed the hope that inhabitants 'nigh to' the bridge might 'disburse so much as will sufficiently repair the same' –

temporarily that is – otherwise it was foreseen that even a great sum might not prove sufficient in the longer term.

In January 1609, it was the turn of the bridge 'over the water of Cover, neare to the foote of the said water in the way leading between Rippon and Middleham': the bridge there was 'decayed and driven away by the force of the said water'. The following January two gentlemen were asked to view the damage and estimate the likely cost of repair. In 1620, ten years later that is, the court referred back to that order and the surveyors' recommendations, 'in virtue whereof . . . they have certified that the said bridge is in great decaie and that £10 will serve for repaire'. That sum was finally accounted for in October 1623. The bridge was repeatedly in the records through the seventeenth and eighteenth centuries, with ever greater sums being necessary to carry out repair work. In 1639 it was £20; in 1673 £85 had to be 'estreated' on the county and in 1748 the Treasurer was asked to pay £167 15s 1d to the Rev. Edward Place to settle 'a bill produced in court for the repairs of Cover Bridge'.

The records for the West Riding are for a later period and the first detailed information relates to the bridges in Garsdale in 1683. The route was described at that time as the highway from Kendal and Kirkby Lonsdale in the west to Middleham and York in the east, although it was 'for foot and horse only'. The report named New Bridge, Church Bridge, Milne Bridge and Clough Bridge and each section contains items of interest. The first to be mentioned was New Bridge, and the complaint was that it 'doth not reach over the whole river when the water goeth over the banks'. At that point the highway was then close to the river and there was a 300-yard stretch that was regularly filled with flood water, to the point where it had 'as strong a streame in it as the river itselfe'. Two possible solutions were put forward – both likely to prove expensive. The simple way would have been to raise the height of the road but this was seen as less effective than changing the route by 'purchaseinge a way through a neighboures ground and makeinge another Arch to the bridge'.

We learn that Church Bridge had the status of a Riding Bridge, maintained that is at the expense of the West Riding, and we can deduce that Milne Bridge was already made of stone since the repairs included laying the pavement, raising the battlements and pointing all the work anew. It is Clough Bridge that is intriguing for it was described as being 'About a mile high upon the moores . . . above a hundred yards from the way ... and of noe use but in a flood'. The river was crossed there by a ford, one 'soe shallow that a foote man may passe without wettinge his feete'. However, in a flood the waters could be rapid enough to make the crossing dangerous and because the arch had fallen down the bridge could not be used. Fortunately the collapse had not affected the piers which were firm enough to build on.

Five years later, 'Garstall Millne Bridge over the river Clough' was again brought to the attention of the magistrates, since work on the wing wall of the bridge had almost diverted the water 'out of its ancient course'. On this occasion also it was said to lie in the highway from Kendal to York, reminding us again of the route's importance in earlier centuries. That importance is implicit in the register of the men who were granted the freedom to trade in York in the late Middle Ages. The rolls cover the years from 1272, before most men had stable surnames, so their by-names tell us where they came from. There were many called 'de Kendal', starting with John de Kendale in 1295, a cooper: five other tradesmen bore that name in the years up to 1349 when the Black Death occurred. Other freemen had the by-names Carlisle, Cockermouth, Penrith and Ulverston. A close inspection of the rolls would see more names added to that list.

One other reference to Garsdale is worth quoting. In 1717, a petition was sent to the JPs at Skipton which defined the road through the dale as part of a much wider network of communications, not just a link between Kendal and York. It passed through the market town of Sedbergh of course and so opened up routes to all 'the north west parts of Lancashire and Cumberland'. To the east it reached Richmond via Askrigg and Middleham and gave access also to 'the towns of Rippon, Wetherby, Knaresborough [and] Borrowbridge'. We know from the earlier reports that it was much used by horses, and this petition emphasises the great number of 'horse packs' that were 'daily con- veyed' along the road, transporting tobacco, sugar, groceries and stockings. It is a reminder of the stocking trade in that part of the county.

SOME WHARFEDALE BRIDGES

In 1689, the bridge over the Wharfe at Buckden was not in use, having been destroyed in the recent floods, and the debate about who was responsible for its rebuilding raised a number of interesting points.

Among those who gave evidence were Geoffrey Slinger of Deepdale and Henry Falshaw of Buckden, two men in their eighties, but even they could offer little help. The bridge had not needed repairs 'within the compass of their remembrance', and they had no idea who might be responsible for its maintenance. They did say though that it was an important bridge, lying 'in the King's highway leading from Skipton to Newcastle and severall other remarkable market towns'. It was estimated that the repairs would cost £70.

The debate was taken up again in 1708 when the bridge was once more in ruins – to the great inconvenience of 'horsemen as well footmen' who were obliged either to 'stay the falling of the water, or else ... goe over to the great hazard of their lives'. Some local witnesses again emphasised the value of the bridge, although the places they named on this occasion were more local than Skipton and Newcastle. It was, they said, a link between Coverdale, Nidderdale and Knaresborough on the one hand, and Ingleton, Kirkby Lonsdale, Dent and Sedbergh on the other. It was ordered that a new stone bridge should be built, this time at a cost of £120.

The inference is that the cost was intended to be borne by the wapentakes of Staincliffe and Ewecross but this court order was immediately challenged by the wapentake representatives. Their first concern was with the bridge's claimed importance, and there are two surviving documents, a letter and a petition, which shed some light on that aspect of the matter: they point incidentally to the growing importance of lead-mining in Buckden. The petitioners maintained that there was 'noe occasion for a bridge att Buckden' since travellers from Settle or Lancashire, who were making their way to Newcastle via Bishopdale, would use Yockenthwaite Bridge. Those en route to Coverdale from Settle would cross the Wharfe at Kettlewell. More to the point, they said they had 'reason to believe that a new bridge att Buckden would bee very much in the interest of some gentlemen who farms some lead mines there' rather than a 'publicke good'.

According to their evidence these Buckden gentlemen had their lead mines on the east side of the river, but they also had a farm valued at £40 p.a. on the west side, and there they kept 'a gang of horses' which they used to carry timber for the mines and 'oares [ore] and chopwood to the mill', a smelt mill that is. These operations, together with the carriage of the lead, meant that they had to cross the river several times

Barden Bridge. The damaged inscription reads: This bridge was repaired at the charge of the whole West Riding 1676. Ten years later a catastrophic storm destroyed several bridges higher up the dale. (*The author*)

each day and this, or so it was alleged, lay behind their enthusiastic support for a new stone bridge.

KETTLEWELL AND STARBOTTON

On 13 July 1686 the Justices of Peace at Skipton certified that:

> on Thursday the eighth of June last past betweene the hours of one and three in the afternoone ... at Kettlewell and Starbotton ... there happened an Earthquake with dreadful claps of thunder which was attended with great showers of haile and raine which descended so violently from the mountains and flowed out of the caverns of the rocks that in a very short moment of tyme it over-flowed the bancks of the River and great streams ran through the saide townes of Kettlewell and Starbotton driving along with them great quantities of great stones, land and sludge soe that it overturned, carried away, warpt up and made useless, unhabit-able, the dwelling houses ...

Perhaps there was an earthquake that day in Wharfedale, although it seems more likely that what the local people experienced was what we would now describe as a cloudburst. Certainly a draft of the document refers to 'a sudan violent and dreadfull tempest of thunder, haile and raine' which 'did tear upp the bancks of the rivers' and 'rent rocks in sunder'. In whatever way we describe the catastrophic events of that day in June there is no doubt that part of Upper Wharfedale was devastated, for it was not only houses that were destroyed. The flood waters also carried away two bridges and over 100 acres of farmland; they covered another 100 acres with great stones, gravel and sand, rendering it useless. The cost of the disaster was put at over £3,000 and numerous persons were 'impoverished and utterly ruined'.

The court order is not the only document that has survived. One petition tells of the damage to the bridges, especially the one over the Wharfe that linked Lancashire with Durham and Newcastle. A second, from a local resident, emphasises the enormous inconvenience the damage to the bridge had caused him, as he and his workmen had 'frequent occasions to passe that roade' on their way to Richmond. A number of carriers and packmen put their names to the petition, including John Hargreaves, Richard Shuttleworth and Robert Whittaker who were almost certainly from Lancashire. They had been 'retarded in their travels' from places such as Preston, Wigan, Warrington and Clitheroe.

The 'Millne' bridge over Cam Gill Beck was also in great ruin, the whole of the arch swept away, but the problem for the county author-ities was to establish who might be responsible for its repair. It was not a Riding Bridge, unlike the bridge over the Wharfe, and the witnesses who were called on to give evidence could not help. Humphrey Topham, aged eighty-five, claimed to have been familiar with the bridge for seventy-five years, but 'never knew who erected or repaired the same'. Similar evidence was given by John Symondson, aged seventy-eight, and he also quoted his father who had 'lived to the age of one hundreth yeares'.

A much later petition makes it clear that the damage caused to some local bridges had not been dealt with immediately. Early in 1694 the inhabitants of several townships in Upper Wharfedale called on the authorities to do something about a small stone bridge in Starbotton, that had also been 'taken downe the streame' about seven years previously. It had been, they said, a bridge 'over which horses might safely passe' and they were requesting a gratuity towards its repair. The 'earthquake' was now passing into the folk lore of the dale, remembered as an inundation 'soe great ... that many of the houses in

Kettlewell about a century ago, with the bridge on the extreme left. This part of the valley was devastated in 1686 when a violent storm destroyed the bridge, fields and numerous buildings. (*Author's collection*)

Starbotton were taken away by the water ... to the utter ruine of severall inhabitants'.

We can obtain a more objective picture of how great that devastation had been from a number of items among the papers in the Quarter Sessions rolls. The names are given there of all the families affected, over thirty in number, together with details of the land and property destroyed, workmen's estimates for the cost of rebuilding, and item-ised inventories of the goods of certain individuals. Among the buildings listed were a mill, houses, lathes, stables and several work-shops, ranging from Jennet Calvert's 'porch, carried away by the water', valued at just over £4, to 'the fire house and other buildings' of Mr Robert Ward, valued at £143. Some of these buildings had been completely destroyed, whereas others were described as 'in danger of being uselesse'.

The account for James Sidgwick's losses contains details of cash, crops, furniture, linen, clothing, farm implements, tools, and house-hold items that ranged from a frying pan to a spinning wheel. There are several entries of real interest, including: '1 ark and 1 panneld chest; whalebone buttons, silk and facinge; a half stone of skinne wool;

1 brandrith, 1 smoothing iron; 3 hundred laths and lyme'. However, the longest and most fascinating inventory is that for Mr Robert Ward, mentioned earlier:

	£	s	d
14 iron rings 6 pair of middle boards	1	6	3
1 stone sled 2 yardes of hay 3 tar cartes	1	12	6
1 stone cart 1 turf cart & 1 coup	0	18	6
2 pair of wheeles & 4 pair of wheeles broken	2	13	4
1 stee iren 9 yardes & ½ in length	0	10	0
3 stirk skins 1 calfe & one twinter stear	2	3	8
1 doz: of gistes shilving for 2 cartes	0	11	6
2 rakes a moldstaffe 2 forkes & a cart sadle	0	6	2
2 barkhames 1 pair of hames 3 backbands	0	4	8
1 barne 17 yardes in length & 18 in breadth	7	0	0
wood to be valued	3	8	0
80 coup full of maynour	1	0	0
One orchard Coulton garth garden at house end			
2 foldes with ways to my houses	30	0	0
7 long stones 5 quarters in length	0	10	6
27 gage of slate	9	0	0
26 cart loades of flagges	1	12	0
5 coupfull of lime	0	11	0
8 oak spares 2 yards in length	0	5	0
Wood bought of Tho: Snell with other wood	6	0	0
2 drags 3 moldrakes & 5 forkes	0	4	6
One new tarpan 1 tarcan & a quarter of tar in it	0	3	6
16 cowbandes 7 boardes 2 yardes in length	0	6	8
6 boardes more 2 yardes in length	0	4	0
4 bearers 2 yardes & ½ in length	0	6	0
1 coupfull of plaistering lime	0	5	0
25 cart load of peates	1	5	0
Glasse windows	1	4	0
Bookes	5	15	0
4 pumps 4 yardes in length	3	0	0
8 turn trees & other grove toolles	3	12	0
Slugeing	1	15	0
9 peckes of malt	0	11	3
Two tubes with other thinges wantinge whiche			
are not above expresst to the value of	1	10	0
In all [sic]	89	18	0

We are presented here with an insight into Robert Ward's many interests, with emphasis initially on the various modes of transport on his farm. There were coups for carrying manure and lime, sleds or sledges for stone, carts for peat and turf, and 'shilving' or shelving, that is wooden boards that could be joined to the sides of the carts to increase their capacity. Of particular interest is the reference to the four pairs of broken wheels, for these were not damaged but taken to pieces, until such time as they might be required again. The entries for three tar carts, together with a new tar pan and a partially full tar can, pose a problem. Of course tar was much used at clipping time and June was the right month for this, but with so much wood listed in the inventory it may be that tar was also being used as a preservative.

Date-stones tell us that this was a great rebuilding period in the dale, and the quantities of wood and stone lost by Robert Ward are enough for us to infer that a new building was going up or that major repairs were being carried out to an existing structure. Boards or planks, oak spars, joists and bearers were separately itemised, sometimes with the exact measurements, and there were also several unspecified but valuable quantities of wood, some of it purchased from Thomas Snell. There was slate stone for roofing, many cart loads of flags, and seven long stones, possibly headers or jambs. Moreover, there was one coup full of plastering lime which suggests that work may actually have been interrupted by the storm. Even the glass windows may belong in this category.

The more closely we look at Robert Ward's losses the more they tell us about his varied activities. The things that had been swept away were of many different kinds, including personal items such as books, malt for brewing, and animals' hides for tanning. More obviously connected with the farm was horse furniture such as barkhams and hames, and implements such as mold rakes, mold staffs and a long stee or ladder. Finally, there were also the four pumps, eight turn trees and the grove tools, all linked with lead mining. We know that Robert Ward had lost his house, but the scale of his plight becomes clear when we see from the inventory that an orchard and barn had been swept away, together with the yard, a garden, two folds and the ways to his property.

Losses of this nature affected individuals, but they also affected the township and the wider community, imposing an enormous financial burden on those concerned. The ratepayers of the West Riding could be expected to fund the repairs to some of the bridges but there was no form of insurance available, so many of the losses could only be made good by raising money over a much wider area. This was done by means of a church brief, that is a letter patent issued by the king which licensed a collection in churches throughout the country. The parish registers of Trumpington, a village in Cambridgeshire, show that villagers there contributed 4s 4d to the distressed inhabitants of Kettlewell and Starbotton, in recognition of their 'loss by an earthquake'.

SKIRDEN BRIDGE

Skirden means 'bright valley' and it has an Old English origin although the spelling of the prefix points to Scandinavian influence. Otherwise, it would now be Sherden or Shirden. The earliest example of the name on record is 'Schirdene' in a charter for Sawley Abbey of 1195–99 and soon afterwards there is reference to 'pontem de Schiredene', that is Skirden Bridge in Bolton by Bowland. This was an

Skirden Bridge. A single arch over Skirden Beck. (*The author*)

important bridge on a major highway through Bowland and it was formerly maintained by the old West Riding. In 1701, the condition of the bridge was discussed at the general meeting of the Quarter Sessions at Pontefract and Ambrose Pudsay of Bolton Hall was asked to survey the site and report back to the court. His recommendations have survived, and the document contains a number of items that throw light on bridge-building techniques at that time:

> Upon the Request of Severall Substantiall Neighbouring Inhabitants haveing viewed the Ruins and Decayes of Skirden bridge Standing over the River Skirden (being a Ridding bridge) do find the Same much out of Repair And having taken Some Workmen along with me the better to inform me what work is necessary to be done att the Said bridge Doe Humbly Certifie this Court that there must be erected att the East end of the Said bridge one new Land Stall one double frame to be Sett under the Said Landstall in length four yards three yards broad and one yard and a half with in the Water one wing wall att the East end of the Said bridge twelve yards long and two yards high, with a frame under the Said wing wall And for bringing the water directly under the Said bridge a Cutt must be made twenty yards long, which (together with pointing and other Necessary works for finishing the Said bridge) cannot be repaired with less then the Summe of Twelve pounds.

The land stall was the site of the abutment which would be constructed on the wooden frame referred to, so presumably there was no naturally firm foundation. The dimensions suggest that the 'double frame' – a rare term – was to be box-like in shape and this would be placed on sunken piles. The inference is that the former land stall had been undermined by the action of the water and that is confirmed by the advice that a 'wing wall' be built up to the abutment, in order to reinforce the embankment. The 'cutt' was to serve the same purpose, creating a channel for the river that would ensure its smooth flow under the bridge. There is little in the report to indicate what the bridge was made of at that time, although the reference to 'pointing' indicates that the repairs were to be carried out by masons. Since no 'arch' is mentioned it seems likely that it was a wooden structure on masonry supports. The sum of £12 to cover the work makes it clear that it was modest in scope.

The 'Skirden River' that had caused the damage is now called Skirden Beck and it joins the Ribble between Sawley Abbey and Bolton by Bowland at the end of a six or seven mile journey from near Tosside. It has given its name to Skirden Hall, just to the west of Tosside, and to a settlement near Forest Becks: there are other scattered farms in the valley and the parish registers identify 'Skirden' as the home of a family called Ellill in the late sixteenth century: they were followed by the Tetleys who enjoyed gentry status. No doubt Mr Robert Tetley of Skirden would have been one of the 'substantial' neighbours who had pressed for the repair of the bridge.

PATELEY BRIDGE

The place-name evidence here is crucial, for the most recent spellings throw in doubt Smith's first suggestion that 'Pateley' means 'forest clearing near the paths'. Instead, the suggestion is that the first element is a Middle English word *padil* which should be interpreted as 'a shallow place in water', in other words a ford. There is a parallel name in thirteenth-century charters for Eshton which has 'wath' as the suffix, a word which itself means a ford, i.e. *c.*1220 'Patheleswathe'. In Pateley Bridge the suffix 'bridge' has not been noted before 1320 and the original suffix emphasised the hamlet's location on a 'gate' or highway, i.e. 1175 'Patleiagate'. In Leland's time the bridge was apparently made of timber.

In *Nidderdale* (1863) the author William Grainge referred to work carried out the previous year on the road near to the bridge at Pateley, saying that a trench had been dug across it for a drain. It had revealed three different causeways at three different depths, one of which was three yards below the existing surface. He surmised that this had led originally to a ford and that the later constructions had formed the approach to a bridge at a lower level. Since little has been written about the bridge it may be worth looking at a few references to it in the Quarter Sessions rolls which have some bearing on what the workmen uncovered.

The first of these, in 1708, is quite brief. It refers to damage caused in August 1707 'by a sudden and violent storm and raine', so bad that 'a vast quantity of gravel, stones and sand was brought downe' and deposited at the end of the bridge, effectively barring access to it. The town street was also the highway at that point, as it still is, and other depositions remind us that this was an on-going problem. A petition of 1741 paints a very vivid picture:

> The inhabitants ... have at very great expense new paved all the town street of Pateley Bridge but that part of the street from the land-butment or springer of the weapentake Bridge adjacent to the said town and over the Nid, for one hundred yards towards and leading to the End of the said town we apprehend to belong to the said Bridge and repairable as such ... not having anything done at it these many years and worn so very low that the Dirt, Water and Sludge of the Town and Roads adjacent fall upon it ... [so that] it is unpassable in winter.

Only a few years later, in 1754, major repairs were recommended. These involved building walls on the approaches to the bridge on both banks. On one side the walls would be 160 feet long; on the other 140 feet long. For the first of these it was proposed 'to draw a line from 'the springer of the arch' and 'make a wall on each side about 4 feet 6 inches high in the middle or deepest place above ground'. These walls were to be covered with broad stones and have 'stone posts set in them to point out the road in floods'. The ground between the walls was to be 'raised and paved ... in the same manner as the town street'.

The workmen's accounts, or parts of them, have survived, bearing the name of a lady called Grace Slater. They include the provision of 'new gates, stoops and rails' together with the labour of two men for 'hanging the gates and putting up the rails': John Robinson and Thomas Briggs were named as contractors. The 'drinkings' they were allowed added 6d to the bill. There was also a payment of 1s 6d for leading a stoop to the bridge and helping to set it up; Joseph Burnley was paid 3s 6d for hewing and setting it.

GRINTON BRIDGE

Elizabeth Berry's work on Swaledale wills provides us with many insights into the life of the dale and her introduction underlines her awareness of the actual and potential value of the material to other local historians. One of the subjects she drew attention to was the number of bequests made in favour of Grinton Bridge, starting with Henry Snawdon's gift of a stirk 'to Grynton brige' in 1522. She noted a second bequest in 1547, four in the 1560s and nine for the period 1574–78, ending with 10s donated by William Collyer in 1591. One or

Grinton Bridge, January, 2011. Leland referred to a bridge on this site in the early sixteenth century. (*The author*)

two of the bequests were of particular interest: Ralph Braydredg of Whitaside (1575) gave 3s 4d for the use of the bridge 'yf it be of stone' and only 20d 'yf it be of woud'. Similarly, in 1569, James Bynkes gave 40s 'if it be beldit with stone'. Clearly, the 'fair bridge' mentioned by Leland earlier in the century must have been made of wood.

The bequests of the 1560s and 1570s are evidence of a significant period in the history of the bridge that is reflected in the Quarter Sessions records. In January 1569, reference was made to 'sundrie summes ... assessed for the re-edifyinge' of a number of North Riding bridges four years earlier, including the one at Grinton. It seems that work at Grinton had begun but not been finished, so further assessments were made which included raising more money, part of an overall total of £564. The order of the court in October made special mention of Grinton, calling for £200 to be collected by the Wapentake bailiffs and then delivered without delay to the four surveyors 'appointed for the new building of the said bridge ... with stone'. Every township in the Riding was expected to make a con-tribution. Evidently, the decision to build a stone bridge had been taken as early as 1565, possibly after much discussion locally and at the Sessions but we have already seen how long it could take to act on such decisions: the Swaledale bequests reflect the pragmatic approach of local people in such situations.

There are many more references to Grinton Bridge, including complex statements in 1584 about the activities of William Gaile or Gaole, one of the official collectors. It helps to explain the delays already referred to in these sixteenth-century projects, and phrases from the order confirm how complicated the financial arrangements were:

> William Gaole charged with £61 8 4, with £15 11 which he received for Grinton Bridge.
>
> Allowing him 15s 6d for gathering of £15 11, so remaineth £61 12 10 [an obvious error].
>
> He alleageth to have paid, as appeareth by particulers of severall bills, £59 13 8.
>
> Mem. That William Gaole is to pay to the Surveyors of Grinton bridge £14 16 att the next Sessions after Midsomer, the which somme he tooke upon him without warrant [to] gather of Whitby Strand and other Wapentakes ...

The collection of the money is of course just one part of a very complicated process. If we take account of the different stages, that is reporting the damage, appointing the Surveyors, meeting with expert workmen, agreeing and fixing the rate, corresponding with the Collectors, arranging for bonds, gathering the money together and handing it over to the interested parties, we are more sympathetic to those involved. Communication by letter, difficulties with transport and meetings of the court at three-month intervals must all have frustrated quick action. If we also consider that each winter took its toll on the structure the delays become more understandable, as does the call on occasion for 'present remedy' to provide temporary relief. In 1614 and 1631, for example, Grinton Bridge was again reported to be in decay; in 1616 a warrant authorised the arrest of William Spenceley of Fremington for failing to carry out repairs.

In a few brief remarks about Grinton Bridge, Andrew Fleming commented on its convenience for people who attended the parish church but he 'found it hard to believe that local traffic was the main reason for the investment involved'. It is true that it was not specifically said to be part of a great highway and we have no accounts of important movement of goods through the village but we should accept, I think, that the investment was in itself testimony to the bridge's importance. Its position on the main route through the dale, as a link between Richmond and Kirkby Stephen, may be what mattered or its convenience for lead-miners, as Fleming himself suggested. When David Harrison discussed the importance of what he called secondary roads on Warburton's map of Yorkshire, *c.*1720, he drew attention to both Grinton Bridge and Pateley Bridge.

Sources

The following abbreviations are used:

SS   Surtees Society
YAS   Yorkshire Archaeological Society
YRS   Yorkshire Archaeological Society, Record Series
YAJ   Yorkshire Archaeological Journal
WYAS   West Yorkshire Archive Service

Chapter 1

M.Y. Ashcroft (ed.), *Documents Relating to the Swaledale Estates of Lord Wharton in the 16th and 17th Centuries*, North Yorkshire County Record Office Publications, No. 36 (1984).

A.G. Crosby (ed.), *Of Names and Places: Selected Writings of Mary Higham* (2007).

J.T. Fowler (ed.), *Memorials of the Abbey of St Mary of Fountains*, SS, Vol. 130 (1918).

E. Garnett (ed.), *Catalogue of the Bothamley Collection* (1999). This valuable series of documents relates predominantly to the Yorkshire Dales and includes the Horton in Ribblesdale deeds referred to in this chapter. It is housed in the Alexander Turnbull Library in Wellington, New Zealand.

M. Higham, 'Lead Mining in Bowland', *Old West Riding*, Vol. 9, pp. 32–5.

I. Kershaw & D.M. Smith (eds), *The Bolton Priory Compotus 1286–1325*, YRS, Vol. 144 (2000).

T. McLean, *Medieval English Gardens* (London, 1989).

D.J.H. Michelmore (ed.), *The Fountains Abbey Rental 1495–96* (Privately printed 1974).

D.J.H. Michelmore (ed.), *The Fountains Abbey Lease Book*, YRS, Vol. 140 (1981).

J. Raine, 'Marske in Swaledale', *YAJ*, Vol. 6 (1881), pp. 172–286.

A.H. Smith (ed.), *The Place-Names of the West Riding of Yorkshire* (Cambridge, 1961).

A.H. Smith (ed.), *The Place-Names of the North Riding of Yorkshire* (Cambridge, 1928).

C.J. Spencer (ed.), *Slaidburn and Bowland: Wills and Administrations*, Vols 1–4, (2000–2001).

C.J. Spencer & R.H. Postlethwaite (eds), *The Registers of the Parish Church of St Andrew, Slaidburn 1600–1852*, Vols 1 & 2 (1994, 1998).

H. Thwaite (ed.), *Abstracts of Abbotside Wills 1552–1688*, YRS, Vol. 130 (1968).

J.R. Walbran (ed.), *Memorials of the Abbey of St Mary of Fountains*, SS, Vols 42, 67 (1863, 1878).

A.J.L. Winchester, *The Harvest of the Hills* (Edinburgh, 2000).

Documentary

The court rolls of Malhamdale, DDMa, Lancashire Record Office.

Deeds relating to Malham, Airton, Hanlith, MD217, Yorkshire Archaeological Society, Claremont, Leeds.

Deeds relating to Kilnsey, MD247, YAS, Claremont, Leeds.

Deeds relating to Addingham, in my personal possession.

Chapter 2

T. Brayshaw & R.M. Robinson, *A History of the Ancient Parish of Giggleswick* (1932).

W. Grainge, *The History and Topography of Little Timble, Great Timble and Snowden* (Otley, 1895).

I. Kershaw & D.M. Smith (eds), *Compotus*.

J. Lister (ed.), *Yorkshire Star Chamber Proceedings* 4, YRS, Vol. 70 (1927).

J.W. Morkill, *The Parish of Kirkby Malhamdale* (1933, reprinted 2005).

J.S. Purvis (ed.), *Tudor Parish Documents of the Diocese of York* (Cambridge, 1948).

J.S. Purvis (ed.), *Select XVI Century Causes in Tithe*, YRS, Vol. 114 (1949).

J.R. Walbran (ed.), *Memorials of Fountains Abbey*, SS 67 (1878).

T.D. Whitaker, *The History and Antiquities of the Deanery of Craven in the County of York* (2nd edition, London, 1812).

Documentary

Quarter Sessions Rolls, Registry of Deeds, Wakefield, West Yorkshire Archive Service. See note on Chapter 7.

Dawson of Langcliffe MSS, Sheepscar, Leeds, WYAS.

Chapter 3

J.C. Atkinson (ed.), *Furness Coucher Book*, Vol. 2, Chetham Society (1888).

W.P. Baildon & J.W. Clay (eds), *Inquisitions Post Mortem in the reigns of Henry IV and Henry V*, YRS, Vol. 59 (1918).

M. Beresford, 'The Lost Villages of Yorkshire', *YAJ*, Vol. 38 (1955).

M. Beresford & J.G. Hurst, *Deserted Medieval Villages* (1989).

F. Collins (ed.), *Feet of Fines for the Tudor Period*, YRS, Vol. 5 (1888).

F. Collins (ed.), *Register of the Freemen of York 1559–1759*, SS, Vol. 102 (1900).

A.G. Crosby (ed.), *Selected Writings of Mary Higham*.

J.T. Fowler, *Memorials of Fountains Abbey*, SS, Vol. 3 (130).

D. Hey, C. Giles, M. Spufford & A. Wareham (eds), *Yorkshire West Riding Hearth Tax Lady Day 1672*, British Record Society (2007).

R.W. Hoyle (ed.), *Early Tudor Craven: Subsidies and Assessments 1510–1547*, YRS, Vol. 145 (1987).

I. Kershaw (ed.), *Bolton Priory Rentals and Ministers' Accounts 1473–1539*, YRS, Vol. 132 (1970).

I. Kershaw & D. Smith (eds), *Compotus*.

K.J. Legg (ed.), *The Lost Cartulary of Bolton Priory*, YRS, Vol. 160 (2009).

D.J.H. Michelmore, *Fountains Rental, 1495–96*.

D.J.H. Michelmore, *Fountains Lease Book*.

P.H. Reaney & R.M. Wilson, *A Dictionary of English Surnames* (Oxford, 1997).

R.H. Skaife (ed.), *Kirkby's Inquest & the Nomina Villarum*, SS, Vol. 49 (1867).

J. Titford, *Penguin Dictionary of British Surnames* (2009).

Documentary

Kirkby Malzeard Deeds and the Elsley family, MD 14 to MD 17, Claremont, Leeds, WYAS.

Quarter Sessions Rolls are the source of anecdotes quoted in the accounts of Nussey House

Chapter 4

S. Archer, *The British 19th Century Surname Atlas* (2003). A CD which maps the distribution of surnames and first names in the 1881 census.

E.K. Berry (ed.), *Swaledale Wills and Inventories 1522–1600*, YRS, Vol. 152 (1998).

W. Brown (ed.), *Yorkshire Deeds*, YRS, Vol. 39 (1909).

A.S. Ellis (ed.), 'Yorkshire Deeds', *YAJ*, Vol. 12 (1893).

J.T. Fowler (ed.), *The Coucher Book of Selby* 2, YRS, Vol. 13 (1883).

R.W. Hoyle, *Tudor Subsidies*.

R.A. McKinley, *The Surnames of Lancashire*, English Surnames Series, Vol. 4 (1981).

J.W.R. Parker (ed.), 'Lay Subsidy Roll, North Riding & the City of York 1327', *Miscellanea*, Part II, YRS, Vol. 74 (1929).

Chapter 5

M.Y. Ashcroft (ed.), *The Swaledale Estates of Lord Wharton*.

E.K. Berry (ed.), *Swaledale Wills*.

P. Hanks & F. Hodges, *A Dictionary of First Names* (OUP, 1990).

B. Jennings (ed.), *A History of Harrogate and Knaresborough* (Huddersfield, 1970).

G.E. McCracken, *The Welcome Claimants Proved, Disproved And Doubtful* (Pennsylvania, 1985).

C.D. Meldrum (ed.), *Abstracts of Bucks County, Pennsylvania Land Records 1684–1723* (Maryland, 1995).

D. Morris, *The Dalesmen of the Mississippi River* (York, 1989, reprinted 2002).

D. Morris, *The Pioneering Emigrants* (Richmond, Yorks. 2006).

G. Redmonds, *Christian Names in Local and Family History* (National Archives, 2004).

S. Smith-Bannister, *Names and Naming Patterns in England 1538–1700* (Oxford, 1997).

C.J. Spencer & R.H. Postlethwaite (eds), *Slaidburn Parish Registers*.

E.G. Withycombe, *The Oxford Dictionary of English Christian Names* (3rd ed. 1977).

Chapter 6

J. Asher, 'Samuel Watson of Knight Stainforth Hall', *North Craven Heritage Trust Journal* (2009), pp. 22–6.

P.W. Coldham, *Emigrants from England to the American Colonies 1773–1776* (USA, 1988).

B. DeWolfe, *Discoveries of America: Personal Accounts of British Emigrants to North America during the Revolutionary Era* (Cambridge, 1997).

R.W. Hoyle (ed.), *Tudor Subsidies*.

R.W. Hoyle (ed.), *Lord Thanet's Benefaction to the Poor of Craven in 1685* (1978).

I. Kershaw (ed.), *Bolton Priory Rentals*.

H. King & A. Harris (eds), *A Survey of the Manor of Settrington*, YRS, Vol. 126 (1962).

R.A. McKinley, *The Surnames of Lancashire*, English Surnames Series IV (1981).

C.D. Meldrum (ed.), *Bucks County Records*.

W. Nicholls, *The History and Traditions of Ravenstonedale* (1877).

E. Pontefract & M. Hartley, *Yorkshire Tour* (London, 1939).

D. Rooksby, *The Quakers in North-West England*, 3 Vols (1994–98).

A. Longstreth Taylor, *The Longstreth Family Records* (Philadelphia, 1909).

Chapter 7

Much of the material used in this chapter is drawn from unpublished Quarter Sessions documents, particularly the Rolls. For a full description of the collection, see:

B.J. Barber, *Guide to the Quarter Sessions Records of the West Riding of Yorkshire 1637–1971* (1984).

Chapter 8

J.C. Atkinson (ed.), *Quarter Sessions Records*, North Riding Record Society (1884–92). There are nine volumes in this series which covers much of the period 1605–1778. Volume 3 contains details about bridges from 1578 and the contract for Catterick Bridge, pp. 33–7.

A. Fleming, *Swaledale: Valley of the Wild River* (Edinburgh, 1998).

D. Harrison, *The Bridges of Medieval England: Transport and Society 400–1800*, (Oxford, 2004).

M. Slack, *The Bridges of Lancashire and Yorkshire* (1986).

E.K. Berry, (ed.), *Swaledale Wills*.

P.C.D. Brears (ed.), *Yorkshire Probate Inventories 1542–1689*, YRS, Vol. 84 (1972).

W. Brown (ed.), *Yorkshire Deeds* 3, YRS, Vol. 63 (1922).

C. Collinson, 'Enterprise and Experiment in the Elizabethan Iron Industry: the Career of Thomas Proctor' *YAJ*, Vol. 68 (1996).

A.A. Cooper, *Yorke Country* (Luton, 1988).

A.G. Crosby (ed.), *Selected writings of Mary Higham* (2007).

R. Fieldhouse & B. Jennings, *A History of Richmond and Swaledale* (Chichester, 1978).

J.T. Fowler (ed.), *Memorials of Ripon* 3, SS, Vol. 81 (1888).

M. Hartley & J. Ingilby, *The Yorkshire Dales* (Dent, 1956).

B. Jennings (ed.), *Harrogate and Knaresborough*.

I. Kershaw, *Bolton Priory: The Economy of a Northern Monastery 1286–1325* (OUP, 1973).

J. Lister (ed.) *Yorkshire Star Chamber Proceedings* 4, YRS, Vol. 70 (1927).

H.B. McCall (ed.) *Yorkshire Star Chamber Proceedings* 2 YRS Vol. 45 (1911).

N. Pevsner, *Yorkshire West Riding*, The Buildings of England, Penguin Books (1959).

J.S. Purvis, 'A Note on Pews and Stalls', *YAJ*, Vol. 37 (1951).

A. Raistrick, *Malham and Malham Moor* (1947, reprinted Clapham, 1971).

A. Raistrick & B. Jennings, *A History of Lead Mining in the Pennines* (1965, reprinted Ilkley, 1983).

D. Whaley, *A Dictionary of Lake District Place-Names*, English Place-Name Society, Regional Series, Vol. 1 (Nottingham, 2006).

Documentary

Deeds relating to numerous places in Yorkshire, MD 87 YAS, Claremont, Leeds.

MD 217 YAS, Claremont, Leeds.

Index

The index lists major place-names but not all minor ones. It also includes surnames which are identified thus (s). Earlier spellings of names are used in the text but given what I judge to be the usual modern form in the index. Entries in italics are by-names or spellings for which the modern form is uncertain.